sewing guide

essential machine-side tips and techniques

the editors of Singer Worldwide

Heather Brine Lambert has illustrated a variety of books and magazine articles over the past two decades. She also applies her artistic bent to interior and home design. Ms. Lambert resides in Massachusetts with her husband Dave, daughters April and Kara, and an assortment of dogs and cats.

Copyright 2007
Creative Publishing international
18705 Lake Drive East
Chanhassen, Minnesota 55317
1-800-328-3895
www.creativepub.com

President/CEO: Ken Fund

Vice President/Sales & Marketing: Peter Ackroyd

Publisher: Winnie Prentiss

Executive Managing Editor: Barbara Harold

Acquisition Editor: Deborah Cannarella

Associate Editor: Beth Baumgartel

Senior Editor: Linda Neubauer

Creative Director: Michele Lanci-Altomare

Art Director: Mary Rohl

Production Manager: Linda Halls, Laura Hokkanen

Cover and Book Design: Mary Rohl

Page Layout: Tina R. Johnson

Illustration: Heather Lambert

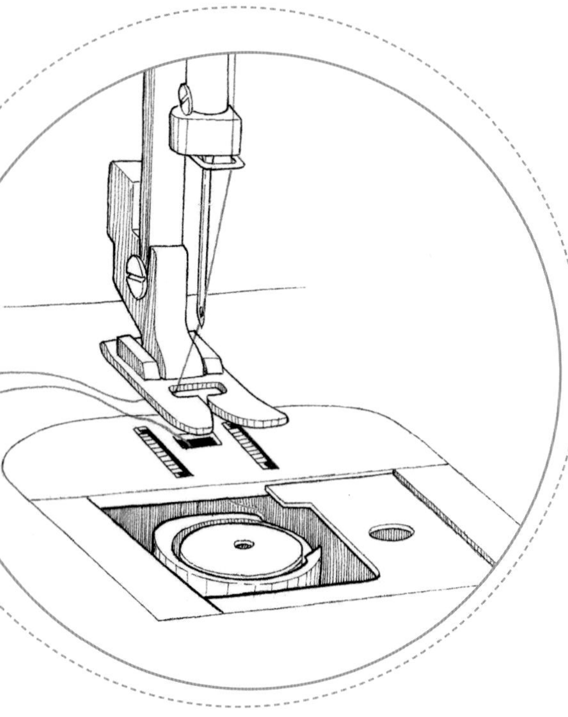

Singer sewing machines are available
at authorized Singer retailers.

Library of Congress Cataloging-in-Publication Data

Singer Simple Sewing Guide :
essential machine-side tips and techniques.

p. cm. -- (Singer simple)

Singer At head of title:

Includes index.

ISBN-13: 978-1-58923-313-3 (soft cover)
ISBN-10: 1-58923-313-1 (soft cover)

1. Dressmaking. 2. Sewing. I. Creative Publishing International. II.

Title: At head of title:. III. Series.

TT515.S6155 2007

646.4'04--dc22 2006032900

Printed in China

10 9 8 7 6 5 4 3 2

contents

inspired to sew?

Here's what you need to know!

Sewing is a practical skill, but it's also a lot of fun—and, with a little help from the *Singer Simple Sewing Guide,* it's one of the easiest crafts to teach yourself.

Singer Simple Sewing Guide explains all the basics. Every color-coded page of this at-a-glance handbook prepares you for success, whether by teaching you an essential sewing technique or by helping you make decisions while you're working at the machine. Keep it handy as you thread your bobbin, cut out your fabric, and assemble your first—or 101st—project!

With clear illustrations and concise text, *Singer Simple Sewing Guide* teaches you all you need to know to get started—and you'll refer to it again and again as you develop your skills and explore the outer edges of your creativity!

If you're just learning to sew, start simple.

You don't need to invest in a lot of tools or accessories. You might just borrow a friend's sewing machine. As an easy first project, you may want to stitch a set of colorful curtain panels or a pair of comfy flannel pajama pants! As soon as you discover how easy it is to transform flat fabric into a fabulous garment or accent for your home, you'll be hooked!

So, take a trip to the fabric store and see what catches your eye! Touch everything. With a little imagination and the *Singer Simple Sewing Guide,* you'll be well on your way to creating your own personal sewing style.

the sewing machine

The function of every sewing machine is the same: to interlock top and bottom threads quickly and precisely to form a series of stitches. In addition to the basic straight stitch, all modern machines sew a zigzag stitch, and most of them sew several decorative stitches, too.

There are fabulous sewing machines for every budget, with user-friendly features that make sewing practically goof-proof. Computerized machines have an amazing variety of stitches and many automatic features. Some are sold with an embroidery module that lets you create professional-quality embroidery at the push of a button.

Every machine is different, so study your owner's manual and learn all the features of your machine to maximize its efficiency and your creativity.

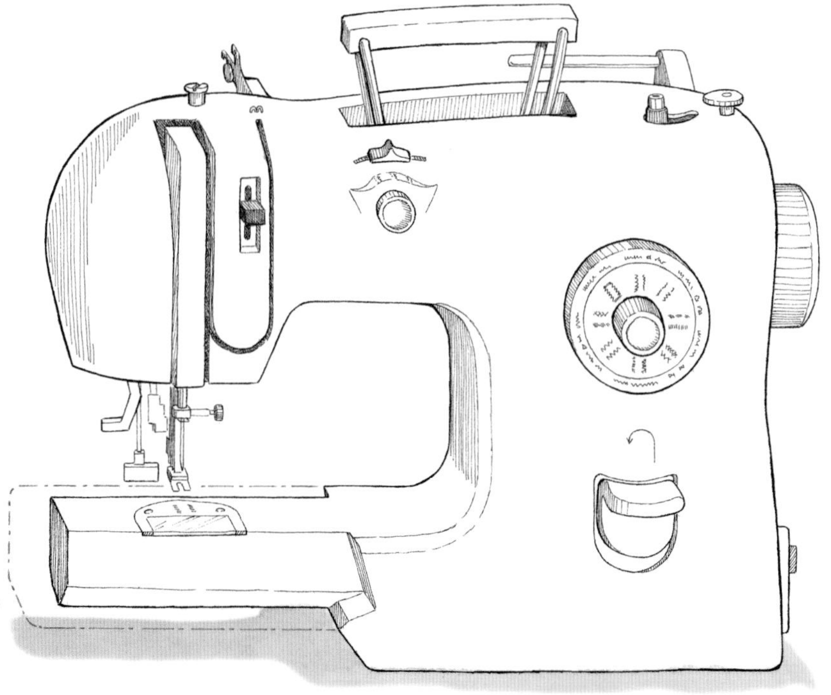

machine features

Every machine operates differently, but they all have similar features, thread guides, and controls. Refer to your owner's manual for specific operating instructions.

automatic needle threader	a button or lever that inserts the thread through the eye of the needle
automatic presser foot pressure	automatically adjusts for different fabric thicknesses
automatic thread cutter	cuts top and bottom threads when a button or knob is pushed or turned
feed dogs	metal teeth below the presser foot that grip the fabric and move it along the bed of the machine
LED or LCD information screen	provides information and guidance but does not adjust or control the machine
low bobbin indicator	beeps or flashes when the bobbin is low
needle stop up/down	presets the needle to stop in the up or down position as needed
presser foot	keeps the fabric flat and guides it over the feed dogs
presser foot knee-lift lever	allows you to lift the presser foot with your knee so you can keep your hands on your work
stitch length and width	adjusts stitch size from 0 to 7 mm wide and from 0 to 6 mm long (range varies by machine)
thread guides	series of guides that control the upper thread to help form stitches and balance tension
throat plate	fits over the feed dogs with an opening for the needle, usually marked with seam allowance lines
variable stitch speed	allows you to speed up the machine for long, repetitive sewing or slow it down for precise, intricate work

machine needles

Always use the sewing machine needles recommended by the manufacturer of your machine. This information is in your manual. Keep an assortment of needle sizes in your supply box. Start every sewing project with a new needle, or change the needle after eight hours of sewing. Dull needles cause skipped stitches and snagged fabric.

The upper portion of the sewing machine needle is called the shank, and the lower portion is called the shaft. The flat area on the back of the shank almost always faces the back of the machine (check your manual). If you insert the needle incorrectly, your stitches will be inconsistent and you could damage the machine.

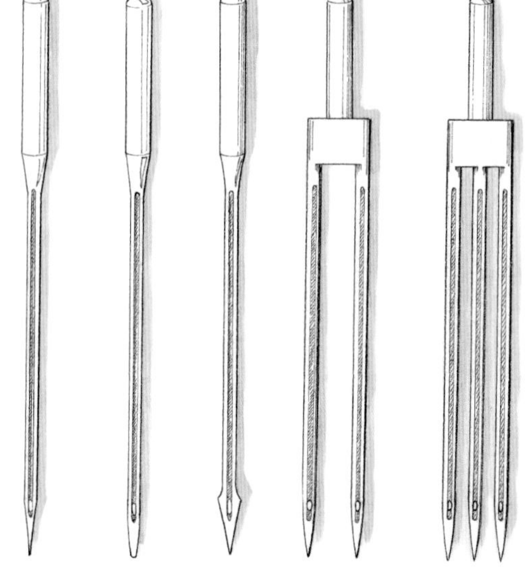

Needle Style

There are four basic needle styles. Fabric type and the purpose of the stitches determine which style you should use.

sharp point needles: for woven fabrics—the sharp point pierces the fabric cleanly

ballpoint needles: for knit fabrics—the rounded tip slips through the knit fabric loops

wedge point needles: for leather—the wedge cuts a tiny slit for each stitch

twin or triple needles: for two or three parallel rows of decorative stitches

Needle Size

Needle size is indicated by two numbers—the American sizes (9, 11, 12, 14, 16, 18) and the European (60, 70, 80, 90,100, 110)—with the smaller numbers representing thinner needles. As a general rule, the heavier the fabric, the larger the needle you'll need. The most widely used needle sizes are 12/80 and 14/90.

If you aren't sure which size to use, start with 12/80. If the thread shreds, try a larger size. If the seam puckers or the machine skips stitches, you may need a smaller needle.

bobbins

Bobbins are small metal or plastic spools that hold the lower thread in a cavity under the needle plate. There are two styles of bobbin: side or front loading, and top loading.

A side- or front-loading bobbin sits inside a bobbin case, which has thread guides to control the lower thread tension. Then the bobbin case fits into the side or front of the machine. Top-loading bobbins simply drop into the cavity below the throat plate (which is sometimes clear plastic, so you can see when the bobbin needs to be rethreaded). The thread is then drawn through built-in tension guides.

Keep a supply of bobbins on hand, wound with the colors you use most often so you won't have to wind a new bobbin mid-seam. Thread the top of the machine and the bobbin with the same type of thread to ensure a balanced stitch.

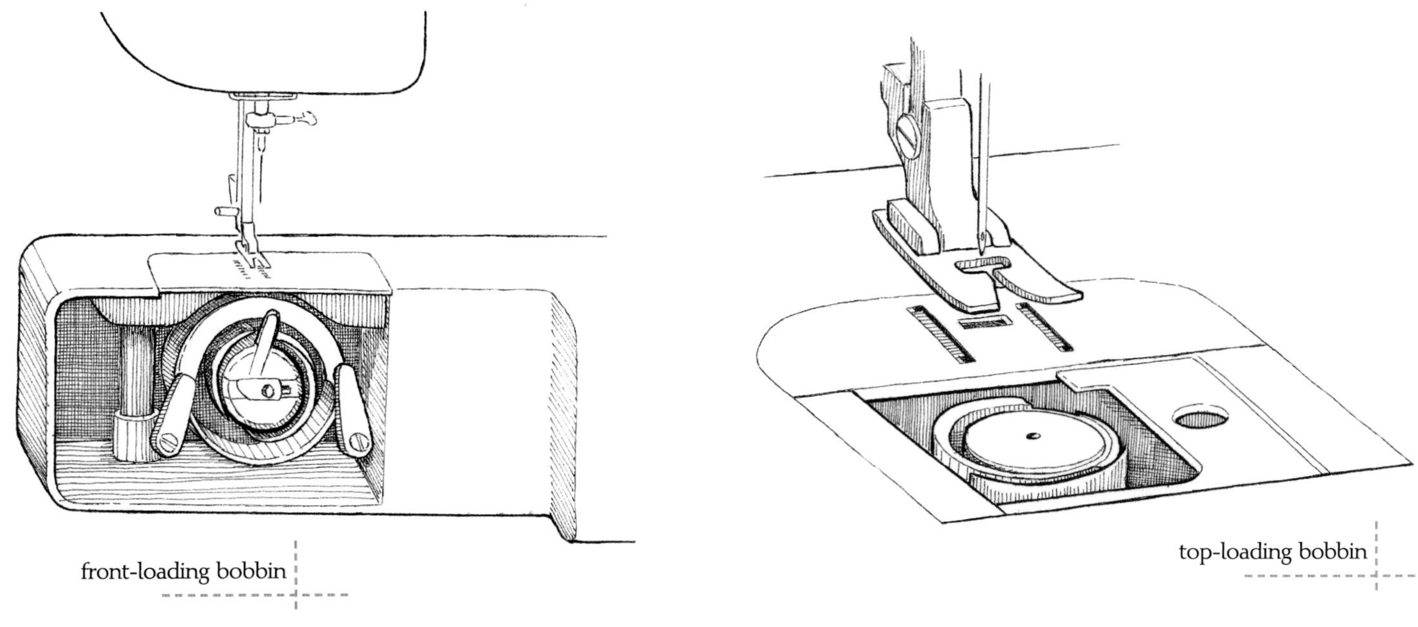

front-loading bobbin

top-loading bobbin

presser feet

A presser foot holds the fabric in place as the feed dogs move it along the bed of the machine. Different feet are suited to different sewing tasks. You'll definitely need an all-purpose foot and a zipper foot, which are included with every machine.

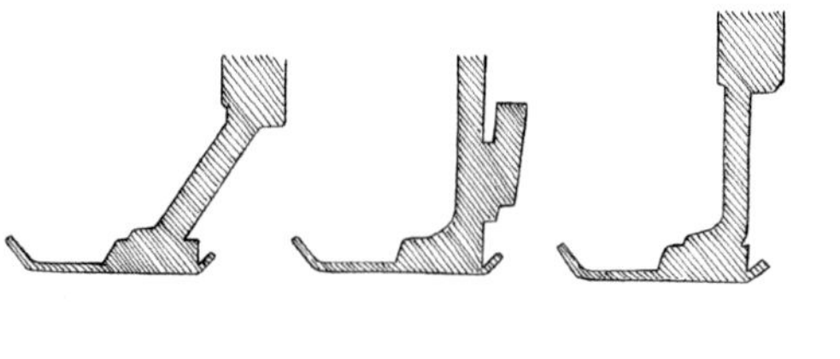

If you buy a special presser foot, make sure the foot shank matches the feet that came with your machine—high shank, low shank, or slanted shank (as shown at left)—or buy a shank adaptor kit to make it fit correctly.

blind hem foot
forms stitches that are not visible from the right side of the fabric

general purpose foot
works well for most sewing purposes, with straight or zigzag stitch

piping foot
makes and applies corded piping

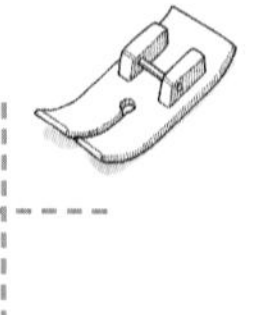

straight stitch foot
sews straight stitches only—good for sheer, lightweight fabrics

buttonhole foot
sews buttonholes automatically in various sizes and shapes

narrow hem foot
double-folds lightweight fabric as the needle stitches a very narrow hem

quarter-inch seam foot
sews 1/4" (6 mm) seams quickly and accurately—ideal for quilting

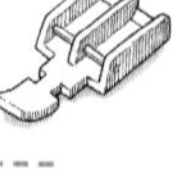

zipper foot
accommodates zippers, piping, and cording

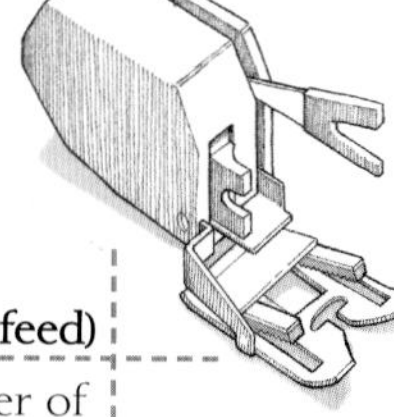

walking foot (even feed)
helps feed the top layer of fabric at the same rate as the bottom layer when stitching several thicknesses or when matching patterns or plaids

overedge/overcast foot
forms stitches over the raw edge to prevent fraying and curling

satin stitch or decorative stitch foot
features a wide, underside groove that glides over decorative stitching

stitch patterns

Even the most basic sewing machine has several stitch patterns. Some computerized machines have more than 500 stitches! Utility stitches are suitable for construction and seam finishing. Decorative stitches are meant to be seen. Many machines also stitch alphabets, numbers, and small motifs.

blind stitch
for blind hemming

buttonhole
for machine-stitched buttonholes, often several variations

cross stitch
for decorative effects

fagoting stitch
for decorative effects or for joining garment sections

multistitch zigzag
for mending and for attaching elastic

overcast stitch
for finishing seams and edges, resembles serger stitch, requires special presser foot

satin stitch
for mending, appliqué, and decorative effects

scallop stitch
for decorative effects

straight stitch
for construction sewing

straight stretch stitch
for construction sewing with knit fabrics

zigzag stitch
for seam- and edge-finishing, attaching elastic, and sometimes for seaming knits

the serger

A serger sews a clean, professional finish on all types of seam allowances and is especially useful when sewing knits. This machine stitches, trims, and overcasts the fabric edge in one step at a very high speed (about 1,600 stitches per minute). With minor machine adjustments, some sergers can blind-hem, gather, and attach bindings.

The major difference among sergers is the number of threads they use. Sergers have either one or two needles and two or three loopers. Loopers work together with the needles to form stitches in much the same way the bobbin works with the needle on the sewing machine. You can thread the loopers with decorative threads for special effects. Always thread the serger needles with utility thread.

All sergers sew a basic, three-thread overlock stitch, used for edge-finishing and seaming knit fabrics.

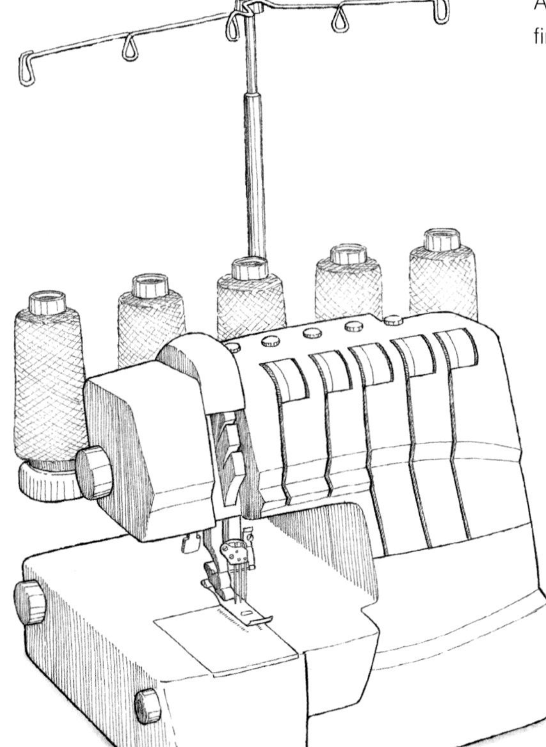

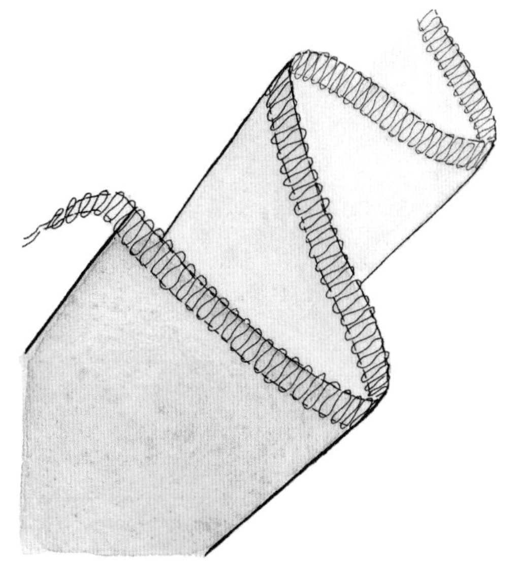

hand-sewing tools

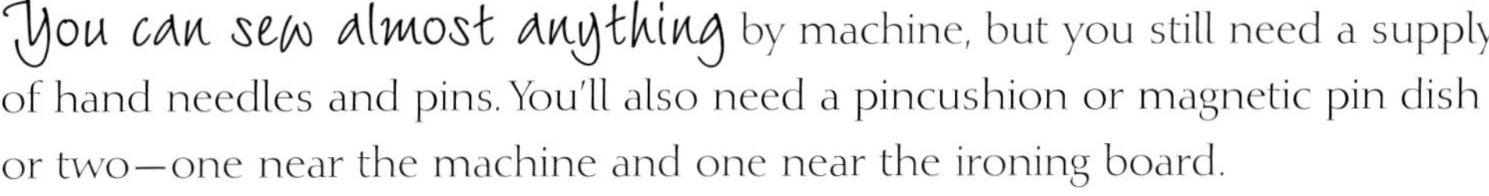

You can sew almost anything by machine, but you still need a supply of hand needles and pins. You'll also need a pincushion or magnetic pin dish or two—one near the machine and one near the ironing board.

Pins

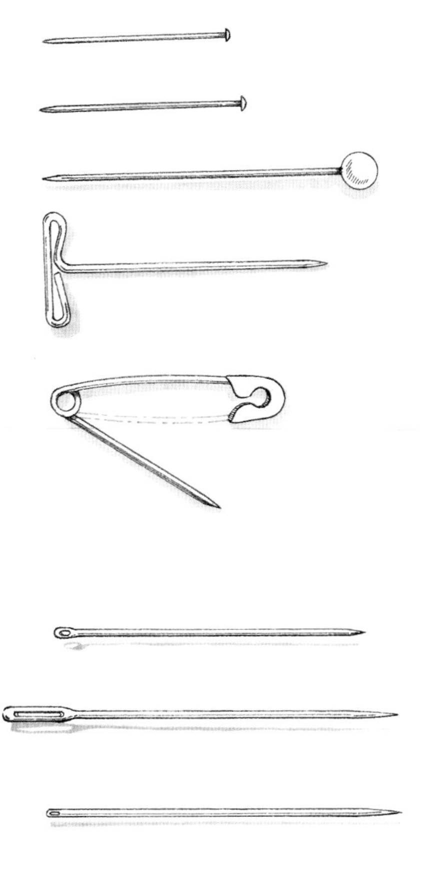

dressmaker straight pins: 1 1/16" (2.7 cm) long, sometimes with large, colored glass heads that are easy to see and grasp

pleating pins: about 1" (2.5 cm) long, used on delicate fabrics

quilting pins: 1 1/4" (3.2 cm) long, ideal for pinning bulky fabrics or multiple layers

t-pins: large with a wide, crossbar head that won't get lost in heavy drapery fabrics and bulky knits or fall out of open-weave fabrics

safety pins: with sharp points that lock into covered ends; helpful when inserting elastic into a casing

Hand-sewing Needles

Hand-sewing needles, sized from 1 to 26, are often sold with several sizes in one package. The larger the needle size, the shorter and finer the needle.

betweens: short with round eyes and commonly used in quilting

embroidery or crewel needles: medium length with larger eyes to accommodate decorative thread or yarn

sharps: all-purpose, medium-length needles with sharp points

milliner's needles: long with round eyes and handy for basting

Rough, bent, or rusty pins and needles ruin fabric, so toss them out.

measuring tools

Careful, accurate measuring is key to sewing success. Once you have cut the fabric, there's no turning back. Be sure you have a seam gauge, a flexible tape measure, and a rigid straightedge ruler. For quilting, you'll want a see-through, acrylic ruler marked with 1/4" (6 mm) parallel lines for quick, accurate measuring.

seam gauge: great for small measurements, especially seam allowances and hems

flexible tape measure: 60" (152.4 cm) soft (but not stretchy) tape measure for body measurements or curved seams

transparent ruler: 2" (5.1 cm) wide transparent ruler with horizontal and vertical measurement markings for easy measuring and marking

yardstick: helpful when you are laying out pattern and fabric, locating grainline, and marking hems

For tailoring and pattern making, there are curved rulers that help you draw shaped seam lines.

cutting tools

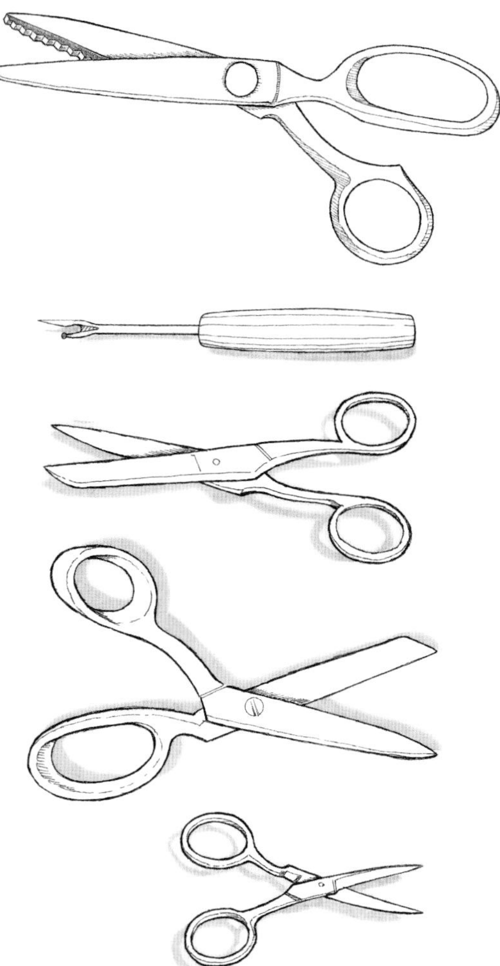

There are many types of cutting tools, but here are some you'll use often. Invest in high-quality tools—it's worth it!—and keep them sharp. Working with dull tools just makes the work harder, and they are more likely to snag or damage fabric. Keep your sewing scissors separate from your household scissors, and never let anyone use them to cut paper!

pinking shears: Pinking shears have zigzag blades that cut a "pinked" edge. Pinking is one way to finish seam allowances to keep them from raveling.

seam ripper: With this precise tool, you can remove unwanted stitches without ripping the fabric. You can also cut open stitched buttonholes.

sewing scissors: You need scissors to trim, grade, and clip seams. Most sewing scissors are 6" (15.2 cm) long with one sharp point and one blunt, rounded point.

sewing shears: Shears are usually 7" to 8" (17.8 to 20.3 cm) long. They have bent handles and a small hole for the thumb. The bottom blade rests on the work surface so the fabric lies flat, which makes it easier to cut long lengths of fabric accurately.

embroidery scissors or thread snips: These small scissors are for precision cutting (trimming seams, cutting corners, and snipping thread ends, for example). They are about 3" to 4" (7.6 to 10.2 cm) long with two sharp points. Some sewers wear them around their necks on a ribbon or string to keep them handy.

Work a seam ripper on the outside of the seam, not between the layers of fabrics. Slide the sharp point under the stitch to cut. Repeat every 1" (2.5 cm) along the seam.

marking tools

Marking tools allow you to transfer symbols and other information from the sewing pattern onto the fabric. These temporary marks help you accurately assemble the fabric pieces after you remove the pattern. Test any marking tool on a scrap of your fabric first to make sure the marks will come off later and won't harm the fabric.

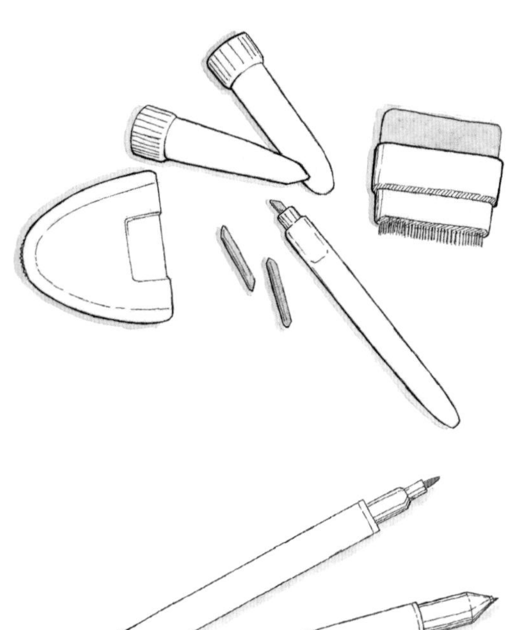

chalk wedge or pencil: With these tools, it's simple to accurately copy design lines and construction markings. Chalk rubs off easily, so mark the fabric just before you're ready to sew.

fabric-marking pens: Water-soluble ink pens usually have blue ink that you can remove from the fabric with a damp sponge when you no longer need the markings. (Do not use water-soluble pens on very lightweight fabrics or on fabrics that need to be dry-cleaned.) Air-soluble ink simply disappears on its own within 48 hours.

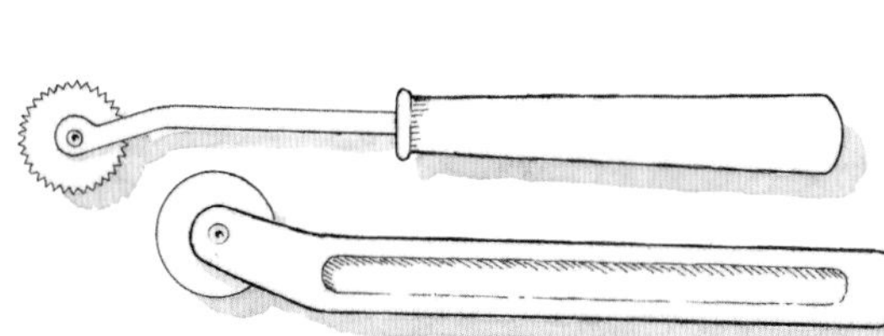

tracing wheel and tracing paper: A tracing wheel has either a smooth edge, which is best for delicate fabrics, or a notched edge, which works well for most other fabrics. The wheel is used with dressmaker's tracing paper to mark large areas and long seam lines. The paper has colored wax on one side and is positioned on the fabric with the wax side down. Roll the tracing wheel over the paper, to transfer the marks. Choose a wax color that is a shade or two different from your fabric so it is clearly visible.

The sharp edge of a sliver of dry bath soap makes an excellent marking tool! Carefully shave it with a knife if you need a finer line.

all about thread

High-quality thread might be your most important sewing tool! It should be smooth and strong with uniform thickness. Color is the most obvious difference between threads, but fiber content is equally important. As a general rule, match the fiber content of the thread with that of the fabric. Use the same type of thread in the needle and in the bobbin (unless sewing with decorative thread).

Common Threads			
Cotton-wrapped polyester thread	**Cotton thread**	**Polyester thread**	**Silk thread**
• general-purpose thread • used for most sewing and dressmaking • suitable for natural or man-made fibers, knit or woven fabrics	• best with cotton, linen, or wool fibers • good with woven fabrics	• suitable for fabrics made of man-made fibers, especially knits	• expensive • suitable for garment sewing on silk and wool fabric

Specialty Threads							
Basting thread	**Hand-quilting thread**	**Invisible thread**	**Machine embroidery thread**	**Metallic thread**	**Serger thread**	**Topstitching thread**	**Upholstery thread**
• lightweight thread, usually 100 percent cotton • used for temporary stitches • breaks easily so you can pull out the stitches	• has a waxy coating to prevent tangles • strong enough to pass through multiple layers of fabric	• usually nylon • used for mending, machine-quilting, and attaching trim	• high-gloss thread • available in a crayon-box assortment of colors, textures, and sizes • designed to fill a specific area smoothly	• has a lovely shimmer • ideal for decorative stitching	• sold on large cones • designed for high-speed sewing • decorative threads, such as wooly nylon, nylon, metallic, cotton, and rayon, can be threaded in loopers	• strong and heavy • produces a well-defined stitch • works well for sewing on buttons	• 100 percent nylon or polyester • strong and resistant to chemicals and mildew • suitable for upholstery fabrics

pressing tools

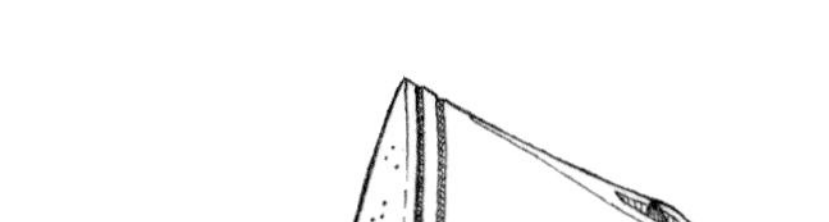

Pressing is the key to professional-looking projects—every step of the way. Pressing and ironing are different processes. To press, lift the iron and firmly place it on the fabric (instead of gliding it over the fabric as you do when you iron). Take the time to press each seam after you stitch it.

You need an iron that steams, mists, sprays, and surges at any temperature setting. The ironing board should be sturdy. Press cloths, such as muslin or cheesecloth, protect the fabric and the iron's sole plate, especially when working with fusibles. Or you can substitute a Teflon-coated cover that fits over the sole plate.

There are several optional pressing tools to help you press shaped seams, corners, and tight areas.

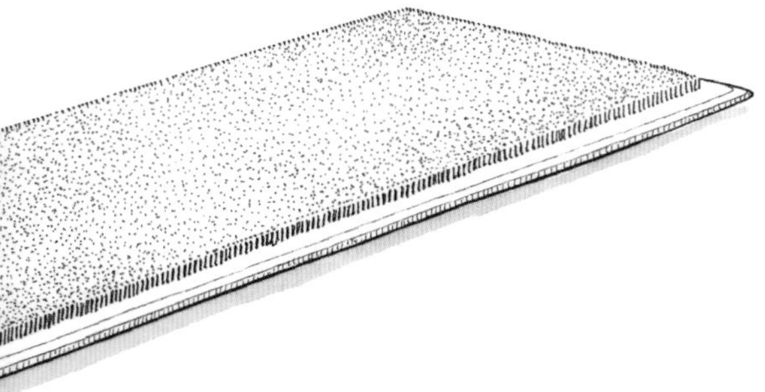

needle board: flexible bed of steel needles for pressing pile fabrics, especially velvet, without crushing the pile (or you can use a fluffy towel)

seam roll: firmly packed, long cushion (half wool, half cotton) for pressing seams open without leaving an imprint on the right side of the fabric

tailor's ham: firmly packed, rounded cushion (half wool, half cotton) for pressing shaped and curved seams and sections

point presser: multipurpose, wooden tool for pounding creases in heavy fabric and pressing different-shaped seams and small areas, such as collar points

sleeve board: narrow, mini ironing board for pressing narrow, tubular garment sections, such as sleeves

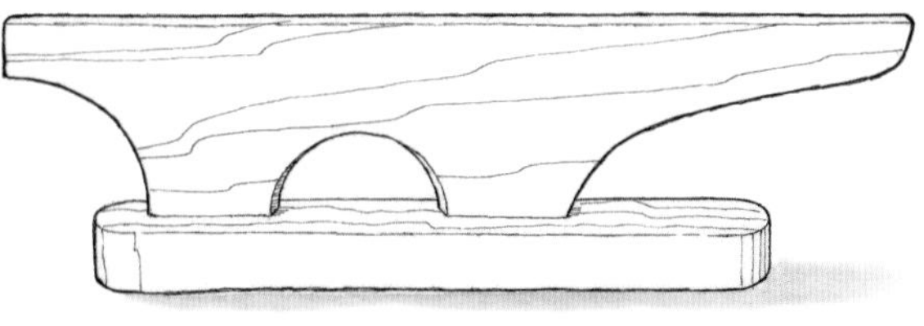

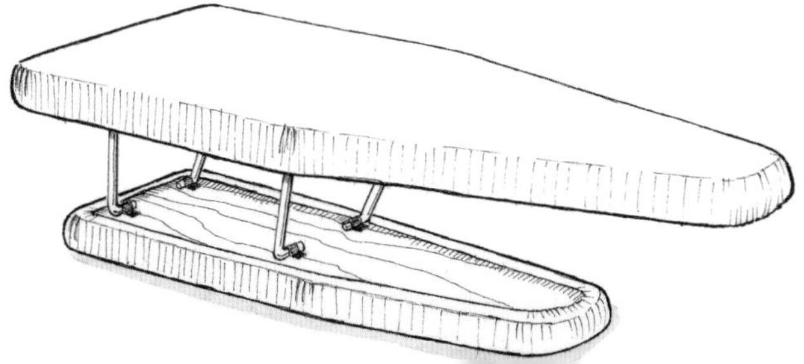

interfacing, stablilizers & fusibles

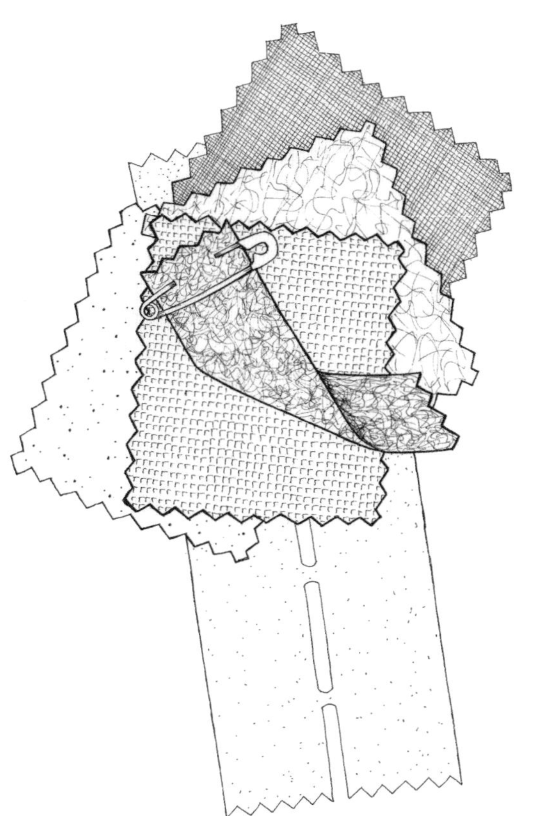

Interfacing is sewn or fused (see page 20) to the wrong side of fabric to add body, stability, and shape to garment pieces. It is used within collars, cuffs, lapels, waistbands, and pockets, behind buttons and buttonholes, and around necklines to prevent stretching. Choose interfacing that is lighter weight than the fashion fabric. To make sure they are compatible, hold them together and make sure the interfacing supports the fabric but doesn't change the way it hangs

Interfacing is either woven, nonwoven, or knit. Woven interfacing should be cut on the same grain as the fabric. Nonwovens can be cut in any direction. Knit interfacing stretches on the crosswise grain and is suitable for lightweight knits and woven fabrics.

Interfacing Type	Uses
sheer or featherweight	lightweight woven and knitted fabrics
lightweight	dress-weight fabrics
medium-weight	suitings and medium-weight to heavy fabrics
heavyweight	accessories, toys, and craft
waistbanding (precut)	waistbands, cuffs, plackets, and straight facings
hair canvas	tailoring

Stabilizers & Other Fusibles

Fusible web bonds together two layers of fabric. It is used instead of stitching for hemming and for securing trim and appliqués before sewing them in place. Fusible web is available with or without paper backing. Hemming tape, which is similar to fusible web, is used specifically to fuse hems. Stabilizers provide extra stability behind decorative stitching. Fabric adhesives, such as fabric glue or glue sticks, temporarily hold fabric layers or permanently secure trim on items that won't be washed or handled excessively.

how to apply interfacing

Sew-in interfacing looks more natural than fusible (iron-on) interfacing, and it's the only choice if your fabric can't withstand high heat. Fusible interfacing has a resin on one side, which bonds to the wrong side of the fabric with the application of heat, moisture, and pressure. Always follow the manufacturer's directions. Fusibles do change the hand of the fabric, so test any fusible on a scrap of the fabric you're using for your porject.

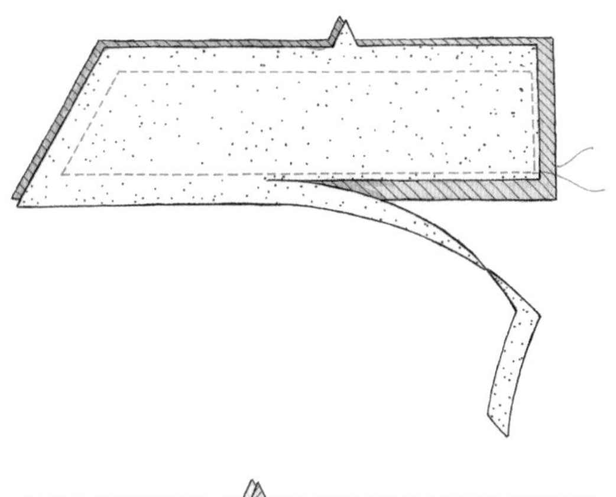

sew-in, lightweight interfacing: Hand- or machine-baste the interfacing to the wrong side of the fabric, next to the seam line, inside the seam allowance. Trim away the interfacing close to the line of stitching.

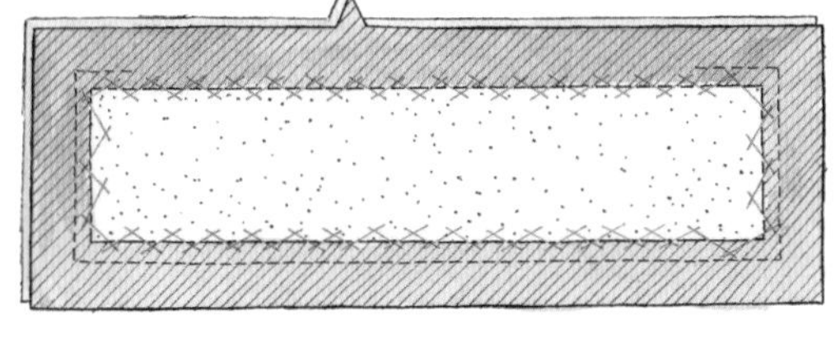

sew-in, medium- to heavy-weight interfacing: Trim the interfacing to fit inside the seam line to minimize bulk in the seam. Hand-baste it to the wrong side of the fabric.

fusible interfacing: Place the interfacing, adhesive side down, on the wrong side of the fabric. Cover it with a damp press cloth. Use an iron on a warm setting and press (don't iron) one section for about 15 seconds. Lift and repeat until the whole piece of interfacing is fused in place.

lining

Lining is most commonly used in tailored garments, such as jackets, coats, trousers, and skirts. A lining prolongs the life of the garment by enclosing and protecting the inner construction details and the interfacing. A commercial pattern will provide pattern pieces and sewing instructions if the garment should be lined.

Lining fabric is tightly woven and lightweight. It has a silky, slippery hand, which makes it easy and comfortable to put on and take off the garment. Lining is sold in different weights and colors and is color-fast, perspiration proof, and wrinkle resistant. It often has a cling-free finish. Choose lining fabric that is softer and lighter weight than your fabric, but has the same care requirements.

What Does a Lining Do?

- makes the garment more comfortable
- makes the garment warmer
- protects the interior surface of the fabric
- hides interior construction details and interfacing
- helps keep the garment from wrinkling
- helps garment hang better and gives fabric more body
- minimizes stretching and wear
- provides structural stability and helps maintain shape
- reduces clinging and makes it easier to slip garment on and off

zippers

Zippers make it easy to put on and take off clothes. All zippers open and close through the action of a self-locking slider and pull tab. There are three types of zippers, distinguished by their teeth: a polyester interlocking coil, molded plastic teeth, and stamped metal teeth. All of these teeth styles are attached to a fabric (usually polyester) tape.

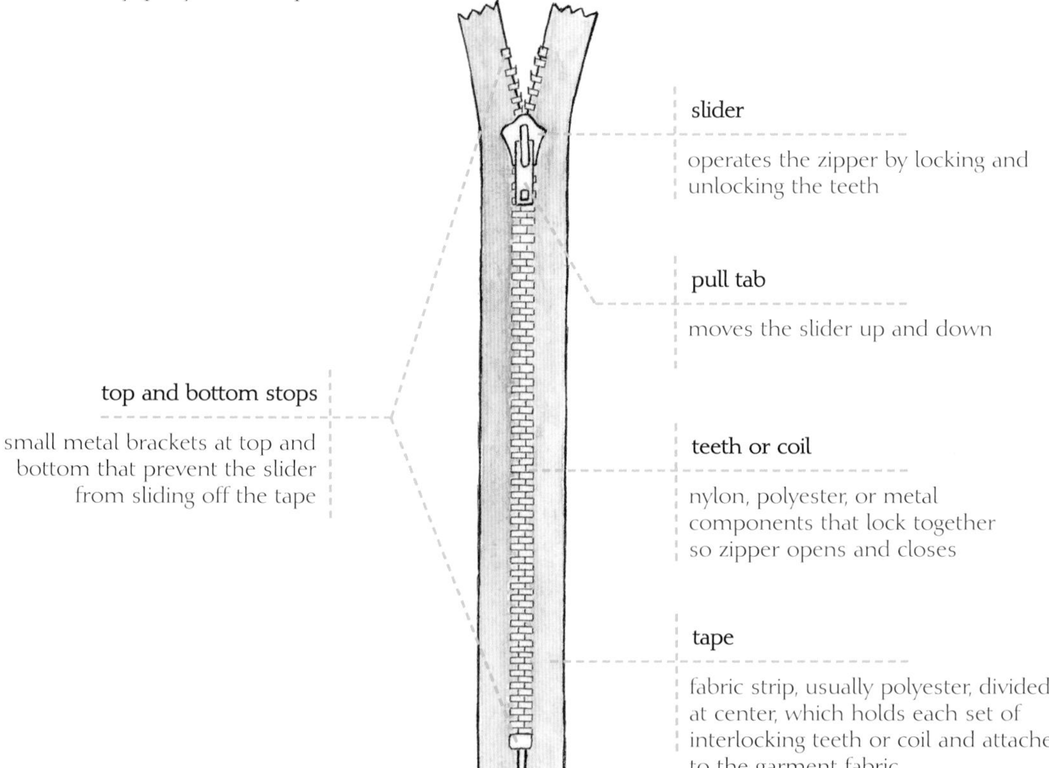

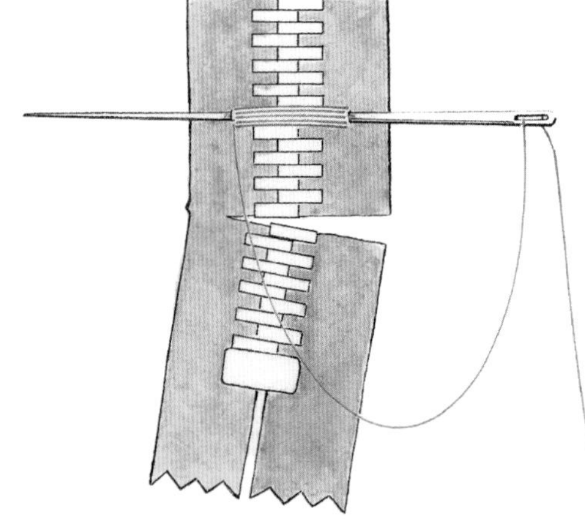

Shortening a Zipper

If you can't find the right length zipper, buy a longer one and shorten it. Close the zipper and mark the desired length. Straight-stitch several times back and forth over the coil or teeth at the mark. Trim the zipper ½" (1.3 cm) below the stitches.

closed bottom zipper

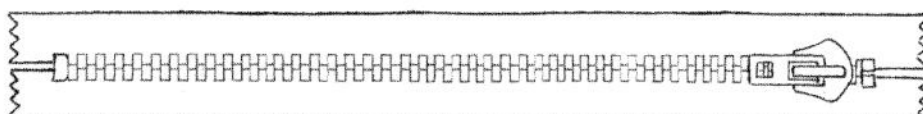

separating zipper

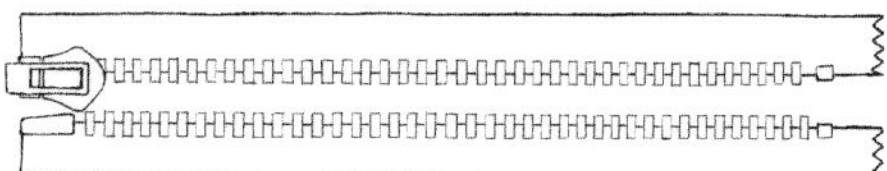

two-way separating zipper

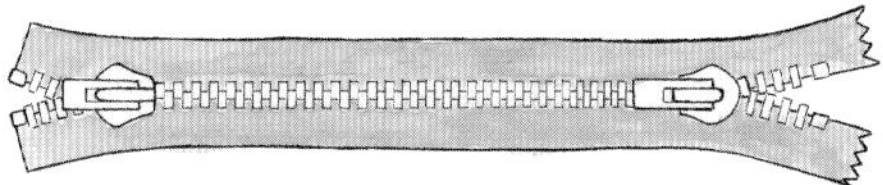

invisible zipper

trouser zipper

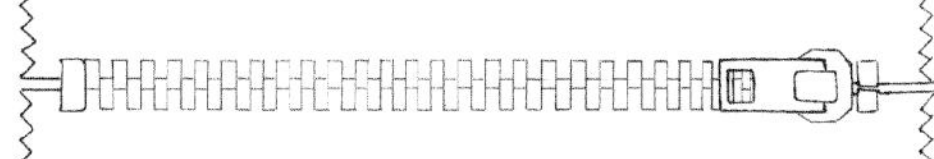

Type	Construction	Characteristics	Uses
closed bottom	coil	4" to 22" (10.2 to 55.9 cm) long; lightweight, flexible, heat resistant	dresses, skirts, pants, sportswear, home décor
closed bottom	molded	4" to 22" (10.2 to 55.9 cm) long; medium-weight, large teeth, decorative, meant to be visible	dresses, jackets, sportswear
closed bottom	stamped metal	4" to 22" (10.2 to 55.9 cm) long; medium- to heavyweight, sturdy, teeth are usually enameled to match tape color	pants, sportswear, work clothes
separating	coil	12" to 48" (30.5 to 122 cm) long; lightweight, flexible, less bulky than metal or molded teeth	handknit sweaters, childrenswear, lightweight jackets
separating	molded	12" to 48" (30.5 to 122 cm) long; medium- to heavyweight, durable, sporty	jackets, sweaters, sportswear
separating	stamped metal	12" to 48" (30.5 to 122 cm) long; medium- to heavyweight	jackets and home decorating items
two-way separating	molded and stamped metal	12" to 48" (30.5 to 122 cm) long; medium- to heavyweight, two pull tabs (so garment can be zipped from top or bottom)	heavy jackets, ski parkas, action sportswear
invisible	coil	9" to 22" (22.9 to 55.9 cm) long; special insertion so it is invisible from right side of garment; requires special presser foot	dresses, skirts, pants, home décor
brass jeans or trousers zippers	stamped metal	6" to 9" (15.2 to 22.9 cm) long; slider has locking feature, slightly wider tape for fly-front insertion	jeans, work pants, skirts (any fly-front design)

buttons & fasteners

Buttons and fasteners are a fun way to personalize your sewing projects—and they're functional, too. Buttons are made in three basic styles, in just about every type of material: plastic, mother-of-pearl, rhinestone, crystal, gemstone, glass, wood, leather, horn, bone, stone, ivory, porcelain, ceramic, and clay. For more about attaching buttons and fasteners, see pages 75 to 77).

Sew-through buttons are mostly flat and have two or four holes. They are best for thin fabrics, blouses, shirts, dresses, pants, and skirts. If you add a thread shank (page 76), you can attach these flat buttons to heavier fabrics.

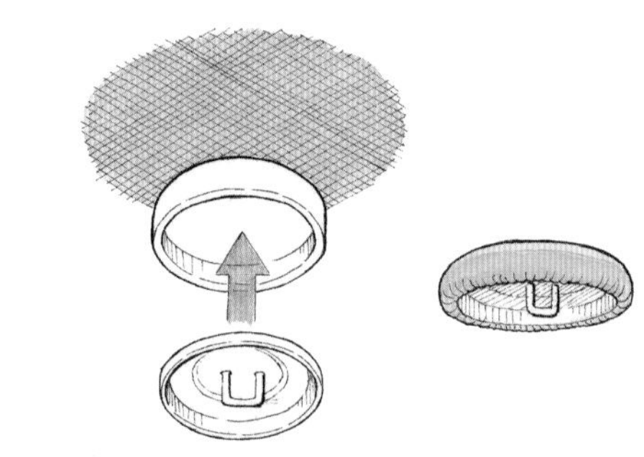

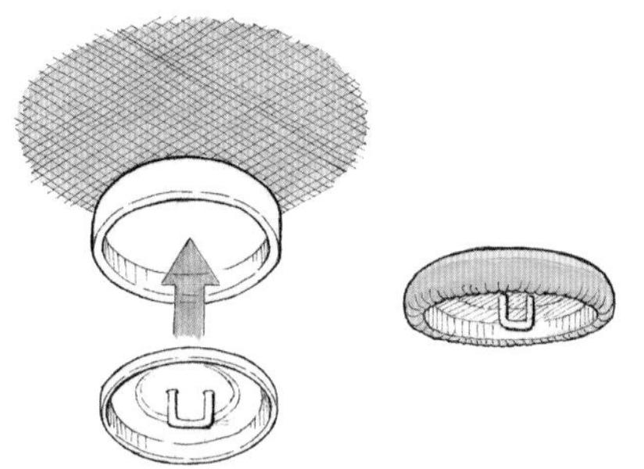

Fabric-covered buttons are sold in kits that include tops, bottoms, and shanks with assembly instructions. Cover the buttons with the fabric of your choice.

Shank buttons have a "neck" that lifts them up from the surface of the fabric. They are used on medium- to heavy-weight fabrics, for jackets, coats, denim garments, and sweaters.

Button size indicates the diameter of the button. Buttons can be as tiny as 1/4" (6 mm) and as large as 2" (5.1 cm).

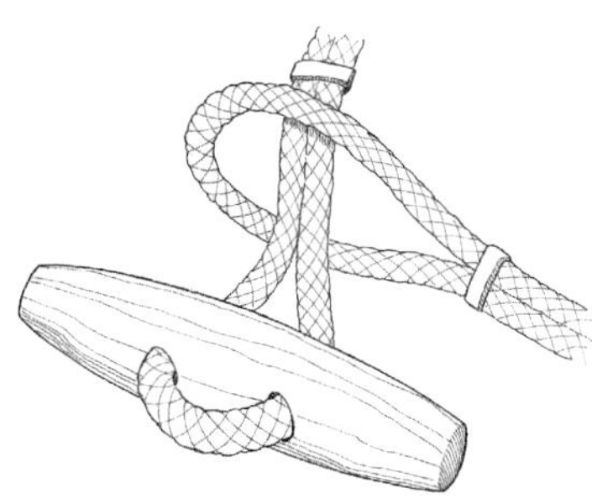

Toggles consist of a cord loop and button-like bar. This type of fastener is effective on lapped closings for a sporty look.

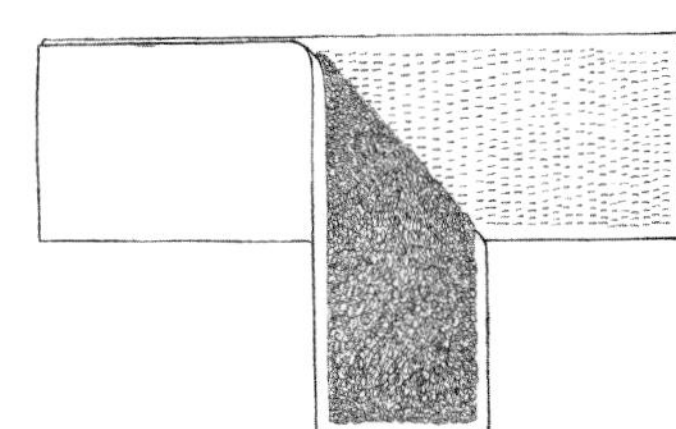

Hook-and-loop tapes (such as Velcro) have two halves. One half has soft loops, the other half has stiff hooks. The two halves cling together for a secure closure. Varieties include sew-in, fusible, or adhesive-backed tapes.

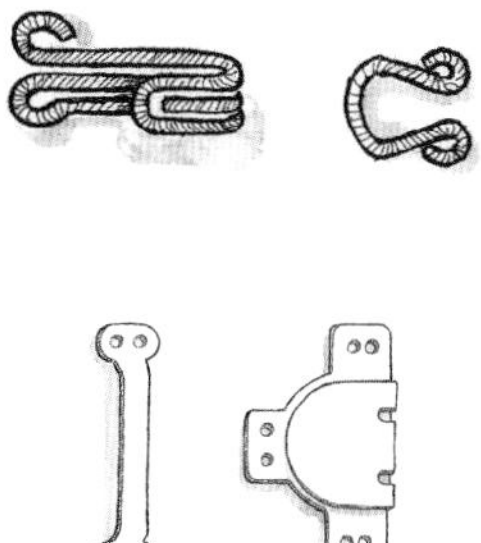

Hooks and eyes come in several shapes and styles. This two-part fastener is used on waistbands and at the top of zipper plackets for a neat overlap.

Frogs are a decorative closure consisting of a pair of loops and a ball button. Those made of cording or braid add unique style.

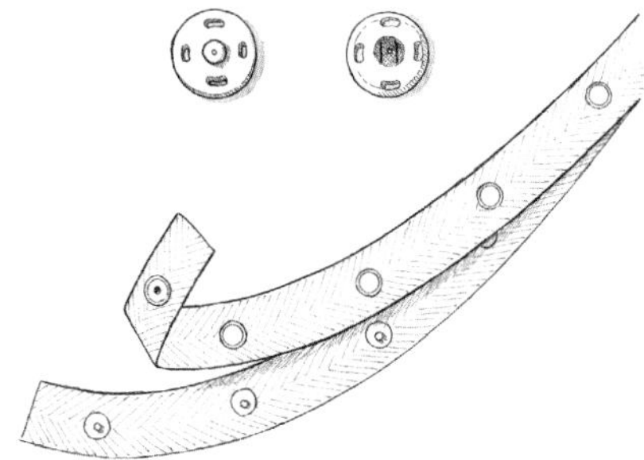

Snaps are another type of two-part fastener. The interlocking parts are a ball and a socket. Styles include individual sew-on snaps and continuous snap tape, shown above. Gripper snaps, generally in bright colors, are a decorative-style snap for the outside of a garment.

elastics

Elastic is a narrow, flexible, stretchable strip that is enclosed in a casing or stitched directly onto a garment. Elastic helps create shape at the waist, wrist, ankle, or neckline (see page 78). Standard widths range from ¼" to 2½" (6 mm to 6.4 cm). You can also buy elastic thread and wide, decorative, waistband elastic. Look for non-roll elastic, which is extra-heavy to prevent it from rolling in a waistband.

High-quality elastic stretches to more than twice its length. Most elastic is a rubber/polyester blend, which can be machine-washed and dry-cleaned.

braided elastic: Braided elastic becomes narrower when it's stretched. This style is used inside casings on sleeve and leg hems and also on swimwear.

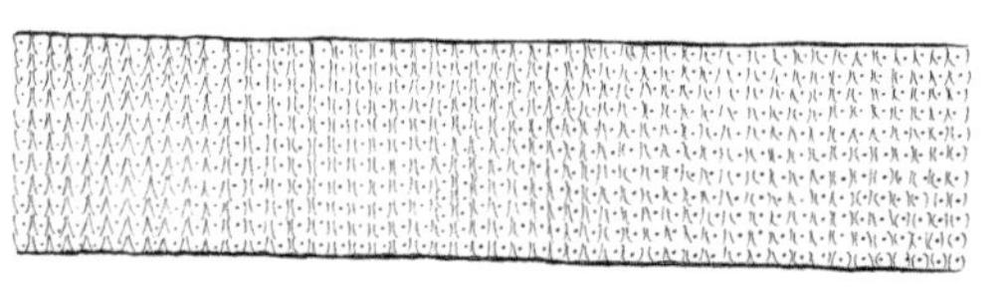

knitted elastic: Knitted elastic is soft and strong. It retains its width when stretched and is good for casings and direct-fabric application on light- to medium-weight fabrics.

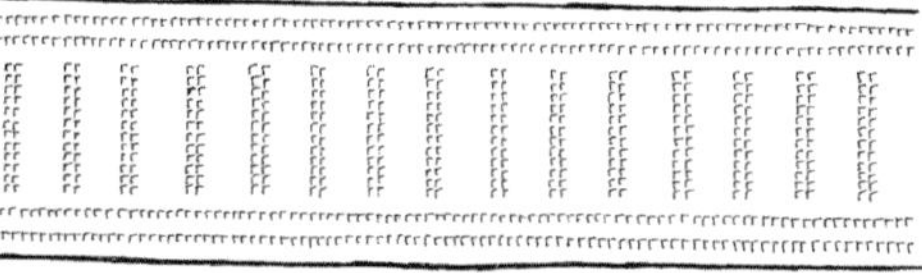

woven elastic: Woven elastic is the strongest elastic. It retains its width when stretched and is good for casings and direct-fabric application on light-, medium-, or heavyweight fabrics.

decorative trim

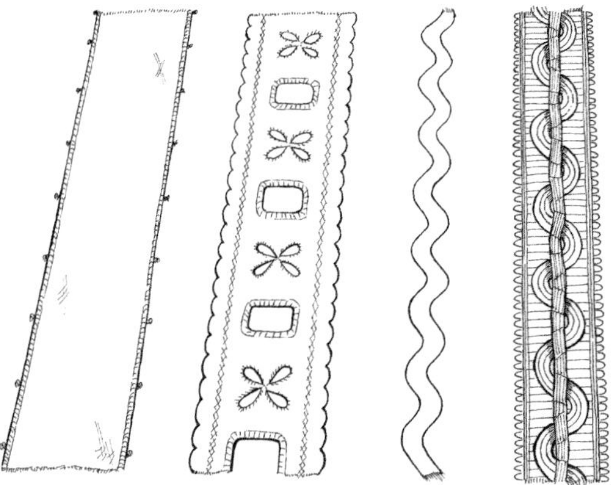

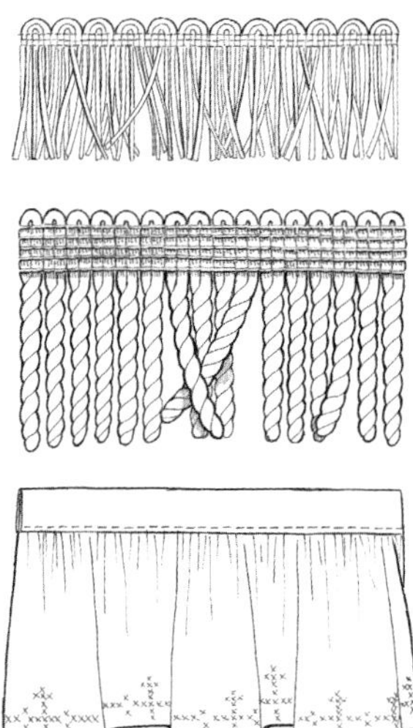

Choosing trim is a matter of personal taste, however, it's important to match the care requirements and weight of the trim with your fabric.

Band trims have two finished edges and should be topstitched in place.

braid: three or more strands plaited together; available in many widths and variations

gimp: narrow braid made of thin cording

middy braid: narrow, flat braid; sold off a bolt or in packages of precut lengths

ribbon: narrow, woven fabric with two finished edges; wide range of widths, weaves, and fibers

rickrack: flat zigzag; many widths and colors

soutache: very narrow braid woven with a center indentation for stitching

Edgings are flat or gathered with one finished edge. The other edge is meant to be caught in a seam or stitched to an edge.

beading: flat trim with openings through which a ribbon can be inserted; can be edging or band trim

eyelet: traditionally white, lightweight, with embroidered holes

fringe: variations include ball, bullion, brush, and chainette; all have a flat heading for application and loose, hanging threads

lace: openwork trim, can be flat or gathered; edging or band trim

piping: fabric-covered cord with a fabric extension for insertion into a seam

ruffling: lace or other fabric gathered onto a heading (extra fabric for insertion into a seam)

Insertion trims are used as narrow, decorative connecting strips between two fabrics.

lace: flat openwork trim; used for lingerie

fagoting: flat strip with continuous crosswise bars of thread, meant to mimic hand-stitched, heirloom fagoting

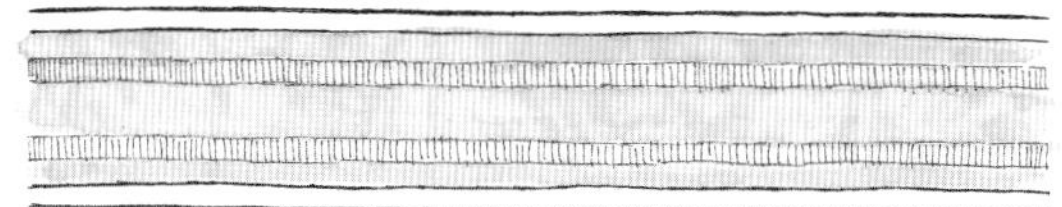

functional trim

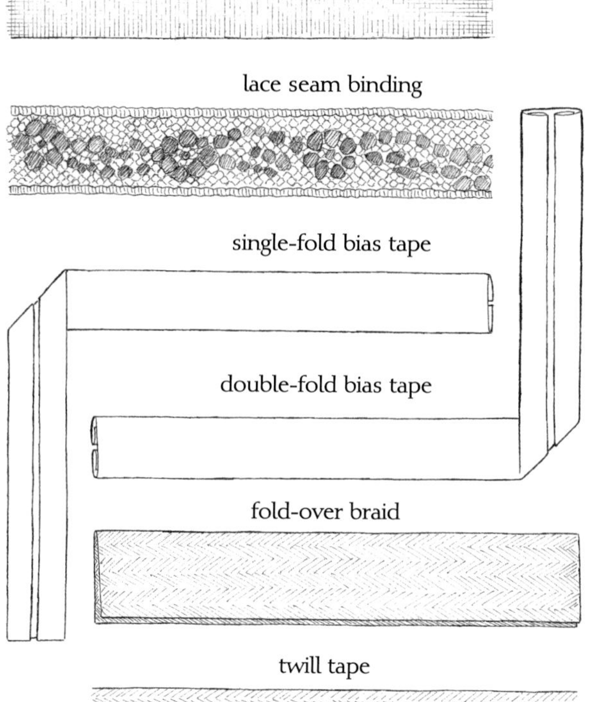

Some trims help with the construction of a garment. They are sold in packages in convenient lengths. When applying trims, mark their placement with a water- or air-soluble pen. Pin or glue the trim in place and sew slowly, easing around the corners. Do not pull the trim taut as you stitch. For more about attaching trims, see pages 83 to 85.

Seam binding is a woven tape, usually 1/2" (1.3 cm) wide. It helps to finish hem edges, reinforce seams, or extend seam allowances.

Lace seam binding is also a decorative trim. It's suitable on hem edges of knit or stretch woven fabrics.

Single-fold bias tape is a flexible, pre-folded tape that is used to encase raw edges. It is simply a bias strip with edges pressed to the wrong side so that they meet in the center. Single-fold bias tape is available ready-made or you can make it from bias-cut strips of fabric (see page 81).

Double-fold bias tape is similar to single-fold bias tape, but is folded a second time slightly off center, so the top is marginally narrower for easier application.

Fold-over braid is a pre-folded, decorative braid trim that is used to encase raw edges.

Twill tape is a strong cotton or polyester tape with a diagonal weave. It's best for making casings and stabilizing and reinforcing seams.

commercial patterns

The beauty of working with commercial patterns is that the hard work is done for you! You are free to focus on the creative decisions—the type and color of the fabric; the style of the buttons and embellishments.

Brand-new pattern catalogs hit the stores either monthly or seasonally. Each catalog contains more than 500 patterns, including a large selection of classic styles and off-season styles, too. So, if you need a heavy jacket in July or a bathing suit in November, you can always find one! The newest styles are in the first few pages of each tabbed section of the catalog and are usually featured in several spreads of fashion photography.

The pattern catalog is divided into sections, each for a specific category: dresses, eveningwear and bridal, sportswear, active sportswear, separates, outerwear, lingerie and sleepwear, women and half-sizes, maternity, men and boys, juniors or preteens, childrenswear, crafts, home decorating, and costumes.

Each pattern has its own style number and is featured on its own page or half-page with a photograph or illustration that shows what the finished garment will look like. There are often alternative views, which show different constructions and minor style variations in length, fullness, decorative stitching, collars, and pockets.

The back of the catalog has an index of pattern style numbers, a fitting measurement chart, and an explanation of figure types and sizing.

pattern sizing

Pattern sizing is different from ready-to-wear sizing. Compare your actual body measurements to the fitting/measurement chart at the back of the catalog. Choose the pattern size that most closely matches your body measurements (see page 31). If all your measurements don't match up with one size, choose a pattern that matches your bust size when making dresses, blouses, and jackets. Choose a pattern that matches your hip size when making skirts and pants.

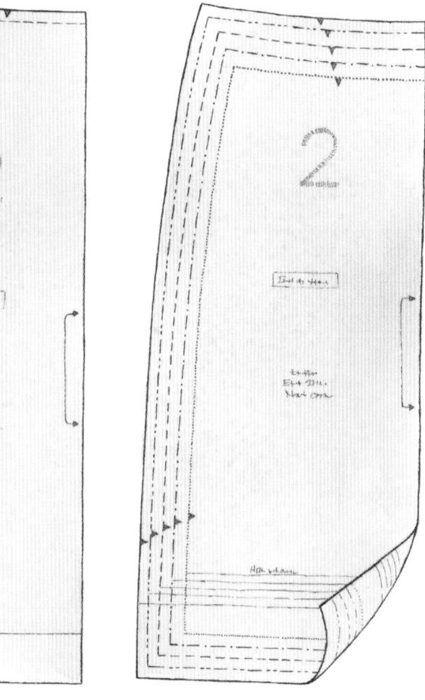

Many patterns are multisize, with several sizes printed on the same tissue paper. If you have a size 10 waist and size 12 hips, for example, you can easily draw alteration lines from one seam line to the other, tapering gently to maintain the garment's shape. Or, if the pattern includes several garments, you can make a size 10 jacket and size 12 skirt. Loose-fitting items are sometimes sized extra-small, small, medium, and large, and those four sizes are often printed on one tissue.

To avoid confusion, seam lines are usually not printed on multisize patterns. Sometimes the different sizes have different types of cutting lines—one solid, one dashed, and one with a dot/dash pattern—to make each size easier to cut accurately.

Multisize patterns are great for children. Don't cut away the larger size cutting lines. Fold them under or trace the size you're making. This way, you can use the same pattern through several growth spurts!

finding the right size

The key to determining the correct size pattern is accurate body measurements. Have someone take your measurements for you, if possible. To do it yourself, stand in front of a full-length mirror and make sure the tape measure is always flat and straight.

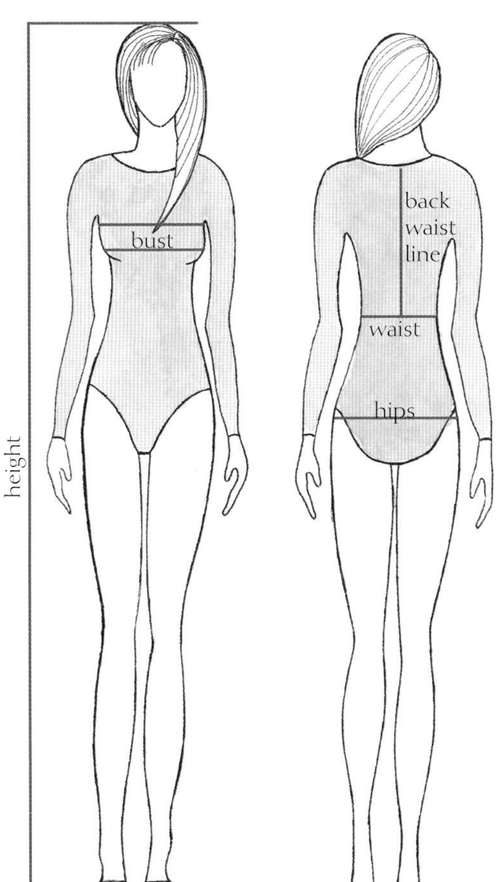

Wear a leotard or underwear and tie a string or ribbon around your waist. The string will roll to your natural waist, making an easy reference point. Stand up straight with your shoulders back. Hold the tape measure snug, but not tight, and parallel to the floor for circumference measurements. Measure twice to double-check. Record your measurements on an index card and bring it with you when you go shopping for your pattern.

1 Bust:
   a. Full bust: Measure around the torso over the fullest part of the bust and straight across the back.
   b. High bust: Measure across the top of the bust, above the full bust line, just under the arm and across the widest part of the back.
      If your high-bust measurement is at least 2" (5.1 cm) more than your full-bust measurement, use the high-bust measurement to determine your pattern size for blouses, dresses, and jackets. If the high-bust measurement is not 2" (5.1 cm) more than the full-bust measurement, use the full-bust measurement.

2 Waist: Measure around your natural waist, directly over the string, around the thinnest part of your body.

3 Hips:
   a. Measure around the fullest part of your hips, usually 7" to 9" (17.8 to 22.9 cm) below the string that marks your waist.
   b. If your waist and hip measurements are not both included in one pattern size, choose the pattern for your hip measurement. It is easier to adjust the pattern at the waist than it is at the hips, particularly if it is a multisize pattern.

4 Back waist length: Measure from the most prominent bone at the base of your neck to the string at your waist.

5 Height: Remove your shoes, stand up tall with your eyes straight ahead, and measure your height against a wall.

design & wearing ease

Design ease and wearing ease affect how close or loose fitting the finished garment will be. Design ease is the extra fullness the designer adds to the pattern to create a garment's silhouette and style. Wearing ease refers to the extra room or space in the garment beyond your body measurements.

Every garment made of woven fabrics needs wearing ease to allow for movement and comfort. A close-fitting top doesn't need much wearing ease, for example, but a coat or jacket does. Knit fabrics stretch, so they don't require wearing ease.

Use your body measurements to determine the correct size pattern. Then consider how the designer intended the garment to fit to help you decide if you will like the finished results. The following terms indicate how much ease is in the pattern. You'll find them in the pattern description on the back of the envelope. The photo or illustration on the front of the envelope will help you visualize the fit, too.

close fitting: little or no wearing ease and no design ease

fitted: minimal wearing ease and little or no design ease

semi-fitted: up to 4" (10.2 cm) of design and wearing ease in the bust area

loose fitting: up to 8" (20.3 cm) of design and wearing ease in the bust area

very loose fitting: more than 8" (20.3 cm) of design and wearing ease in the bust area

the pattern envelope

The pattern envelope is designed to give you all the information you need to decide whether the pattern is right for you.

The envelope front is all about fashion—what the finished garment or project will look like. The back of the envelope provides all the important information you need to sew all the items included in the pattern.

Elements on the Front

- ☐ Fashion photograph(s) or illustration(s)
- ☐ Name of the pattern company and pattern style number
- ☐ Figure type (misses, women's, half-sizes, etc.) and size
- ☐ Identifying logos (such as for petite, multisize, easy to sew, and knits only)

Elements on the Back

- ☐ Line drawings—of the back views and sometimes front views—show the shape and outline of the design, seams, details, pocket placement, zipper location, etc.
- ☐ Garment caption is a written description of the garment.
- ☐ Number of pattern pieces required for the garment
- ☐ Finished garment measurements, indicating how long and how full the finished garment will be
- ☐ Recommended fabrics and information about fabric suitability. Fabrics with a nap or a one-way design require extra fabric, so follow the "with nap" yardage suggestion (see page 46.)
- ☐ Notions are the necessary items you need to complete the design, including thread, zipper, buttons, and seam binding.
- ☐ A body measurement chart may be printed on the envelope flap or on the instruction sheet. It is always printed in the back of the catalog.
- ☐ The yardage block indicates how much fabric, interfacing, and lining you need to make the items in the pattern. Highlight the information for your size and the variation you plan to make.
- ☐ Style number, size, and price

the instruction sheet

Inside the envelope, folded with the pattern pieces, you'll find the instruction sheet, which explains how to lay out the pattern, cut the fabric, and sew the pieces together.

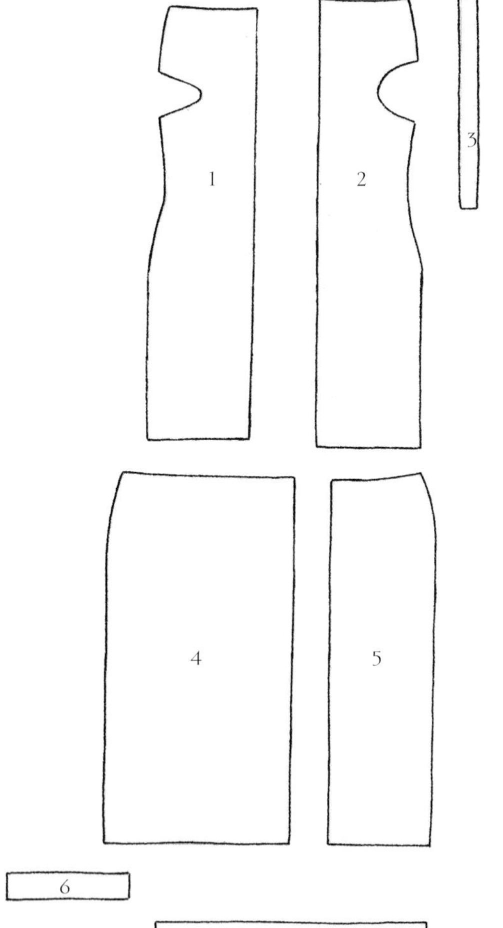

pattern pieces key: This key includes a list and line drawings of all the pieces. The drawings help you visualize the pieces you will be using. Usually there is a list of which pieces are needed for each particular item. Circle the pieces you'll use.

general sewing information: Here you'll find important tips and basic cutting and sewing techniques. This section explains the symbols on the pattern pieces and also includes a brief glossary of terms. Sometimes there is a body measurement chart.

cutting layouts: There is a cutting "map" for every size, every fabric width, and every item shown on the front of the envelope. The layouts show you how to fold the fabric and position the pieces for the most economical use of the fabric (see pages 46 and 47). Layout guides for lining, interfacing, or contrast fabric are provided, too, if needed.

step-by-step sewing guide: This section provides step-by-step, clearly written instructions with construction sketches. If a step is complex, there is often a secondary, enlarged sketch.

Read through all the construction steps before starting. It's easier to get where you're going when you know the path!

the pattern pieces

Pattern pieces are printed on lightweight tissue paper. In the center of each printed piece is a section with general information, including the pattern style number, size, the name of the piece (skirt front, waistband, etc.), and its assigned number. Cutting information ("cut one on fold," "cut two," etc.) is also printed on the pattern piece. All pattern companies use a universal system of marking symbols.

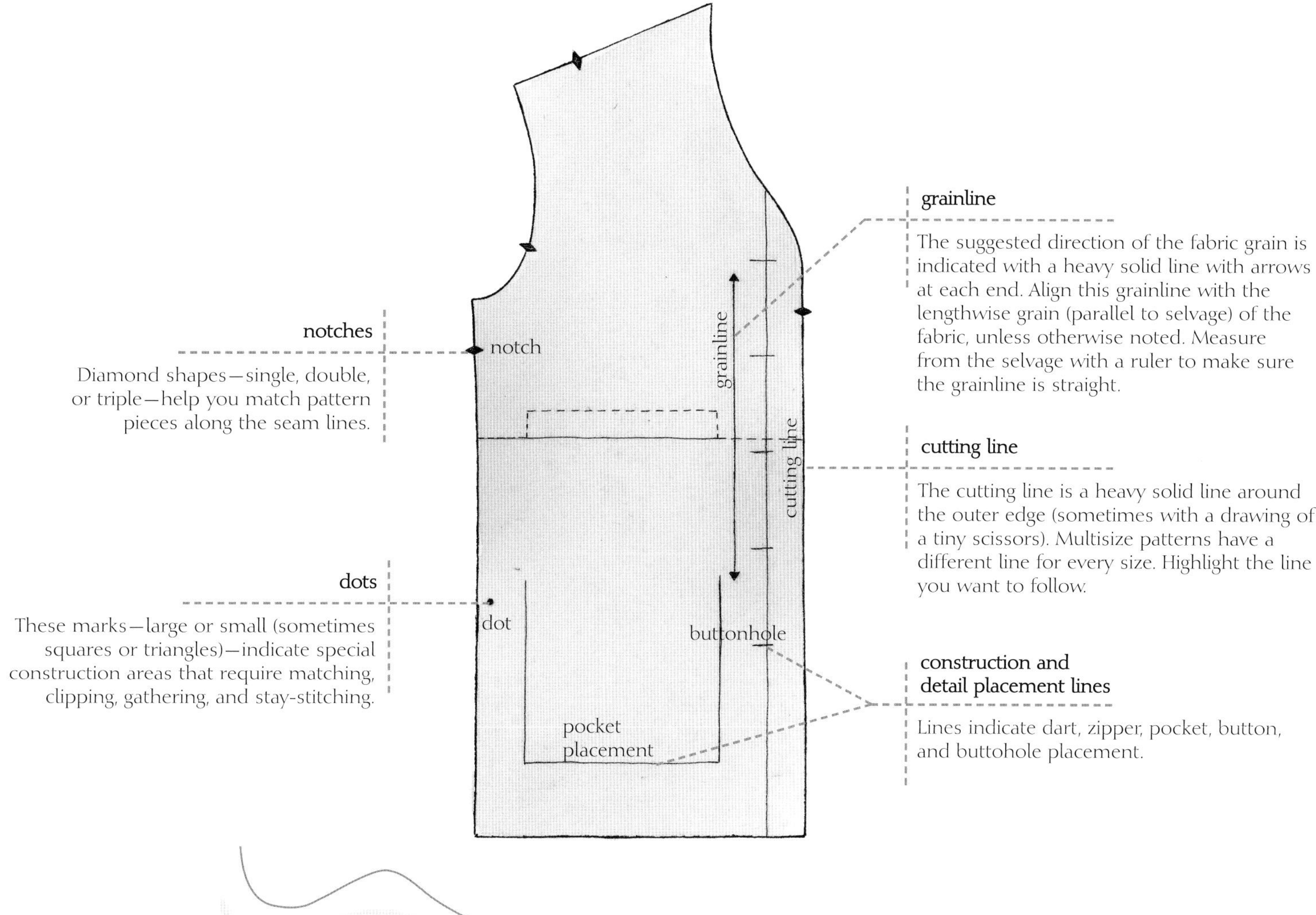

notches

Diamond shapes—single, double, or triple—help you match pattern pieces along the seam lines.

dots

These marks—large or small (sometimes squares or triangles)—indicate special construction areas that require matching, clipping, gathering, and stay-stitching.

grainline

The suggested direction of the fabric grain is indicated with a heavy solid line with arrows at each end. Align this grainline with the lengthwise grain (parallel to selvage) of the fabric, unless otherwise noted. Measure from the selvage with a ruler to make sure the grainline is straight.

cutting line

The cutting line is a heavy solid line around the outer edge (sometimes with a drawing of a tiny scissors). Multisize patterns have a different line for every size. Highlight the line you want to follow.

construction and detail placement lines

Lines indicate dart, zipper, pocket, button, and buttohole placement.

seam lines or stitching lines

Many patterns, especially multisize patterns, do not include seam lines but do indicate the width of the seam allowance. Broken lines, usually ⅝" (1.6 cm) from the cutting lines (or other desired seam allowance) indicate where to seam the fabric.

pattern adjustment lines

Double lines (solid or dashed) across the piece indicate where to shorten or lengthen the pattern.

fold line (interior)

This solid line (without curved arrow symbols) indicates where a piece will fold, such as along a lapel or in the center of a waistband.

fold line (exterior)

This thin, solid line on the outer edge (usually center front or center back) is often identified by a "cut on the fold" bracket, just inside the pattern edge. The bracket has short arrows that point toward the fold line. Place the line on the fold of the fabric; do not cut along this line. Once cut, the fabric opens to double its size. The fold line is positioned to eliminate an unwanted seam, usually at the center front or center back of a garment.

hem line

The solid line along the bottom of the pattern piece shows where to fold the hem so the finished garment is the length indicated on the pattern envelope. If there is no drawn hem line, the hem allowance will be printed along the lower cutting line.

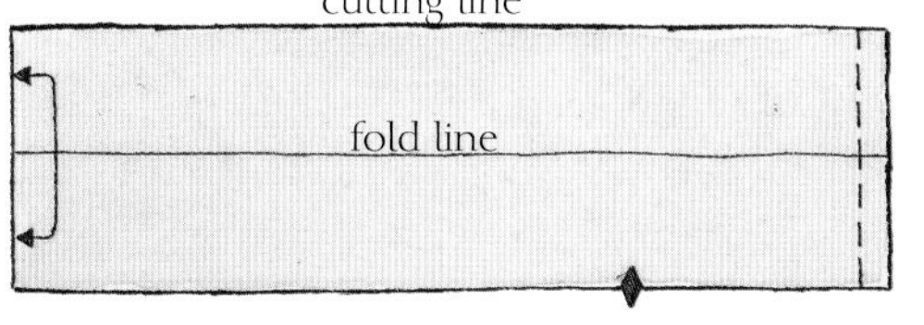

If you tear the paper pattern, simply tape together the torn pieces. Redraw the lines and marks with a pencil or nonabsorbent marker.

simple length adjustments

You can save time and fabric—and get a better fit—by making pattern length adjustments before you cut your fabric. Before you begin, press the pattern piece with a dry, warm iron to remove wrinkles and folds.

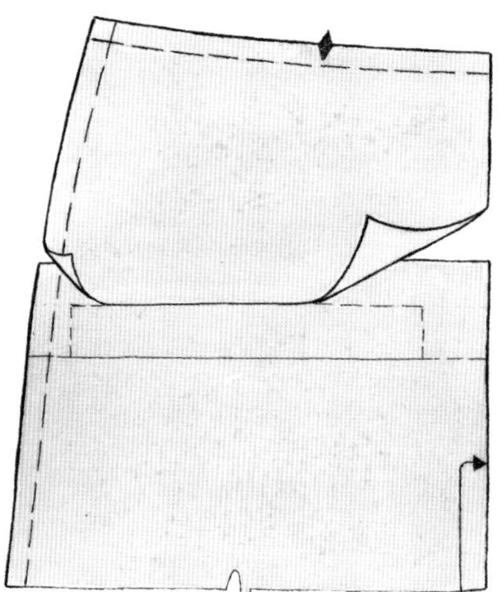

Compare your body measurements (see page 31) with the measurement of the pattern from seam line to hem line to decide how much to shorten or lengthen. If the pattern doesn't have specific pattern adjustment lines, you can lengthen or shorten it at the hem without drastically changing the shape of the finished garment. Simply cut away or draw in the desired amount of length.

To Shorten a Pattern

Cut along the pattern adjustment line and overlap the cut edges the desired amount. Measure with a ruler or tape measure to be sure that the pattern is overlapped uniformly along the cut. Tape the edges together. With a shaped ruler and pencil or marker, redraw and blend the cutting lines. Repeat for corresponding pieces (for example, skirt front and back, both sleeve pieces for a two-piece sleeve, bodice front and back).

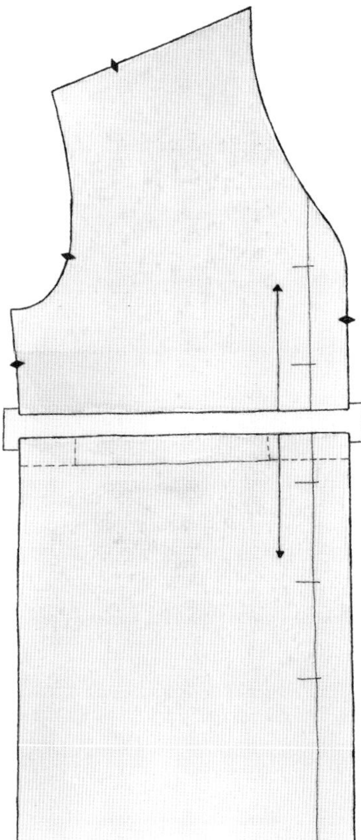

To Lengthen a Pattern

Cut along the pattern adjustment line and place a wide strip of paper under the cut edges (be sure the paper is wide enough to accommodate the extra length). Spread the cut pattern apart the desired amount of adjustment and tape each edge to the paper. Measure the gap with a ruler or tape measure to ensure that the pattern is spread uniformly along the cut. With a pencil or marker, redraw and blend the cutting lines and any other markings. Repeat for corresponding pieces.

choosing the right fabric

A trip to the fabric store is inspirational! From cotton broadcloth to fuzzy fleece, every fabric has its own personality. The way it looks, feels, drapes, launders, and wears is determined by several characteristics: fiber content, construction (woven or knitted), and finishes. This information is often listed on the end of the fabric bolt. (See pages 100 to 107 for more information about fabric characteristics and care.)

Fibers are either natural or man-made, and a fabric can be made entirely from one fiber or from a combination of fibers. Natural fibers come from plants (cotton and linen) or animals (wool and silk). They tend to shrink and lose shape, but are comfortable and absorbent.

Man-made fibers, produced through chemical processes, are designed to mimic natural fibers. They retain their shape and are shrink and stain resistant, but they aren't as comfortable as natural fibers. By blending fibers, manufacturers maximize the positive characteristics of each to create more comfortable, durable, and pleasing fabrics.

How to Choose Fabric

- [ ] Check the back of the pattern envelope for suggestions.
- [ ] Certain fabrics have nap (see page 96) so be sure to buy the extra yardage that nap fabrics require.
- [ ] Consider your wardrobe—which fabrics are most comfortable and flattering?
- [ ] Understand the properties of the fibers to know how the fabric will perform.
- [ ] Handle the fabric and see how it falls over your hand. Does it drape or is it crisp and stiff?
- [ ] Crush a corner with your hand. Does it bounce back or does it wrinkle?
- [ ] Do the edges ravel excessively? How tight is the weave? A tightly woven fabric is easier to sew and maintain.
- [ ] Is the color or pattern consistent across the whole length of fabric?
- [ ] How much does the fabric stretch (and do you want it to stretch)?
- [ ] Do you notice any pilling or loose threads? Fabrics with this tendency may not wear well.

prepare your work space

Organize your sewing space and equipment so you are ready to sew whenever the urge strikes. If you are lucky, you can leave your sewing machines and supplies set up in a space of their own. Most sewers, though, sew on their kitchen or dining room tables.

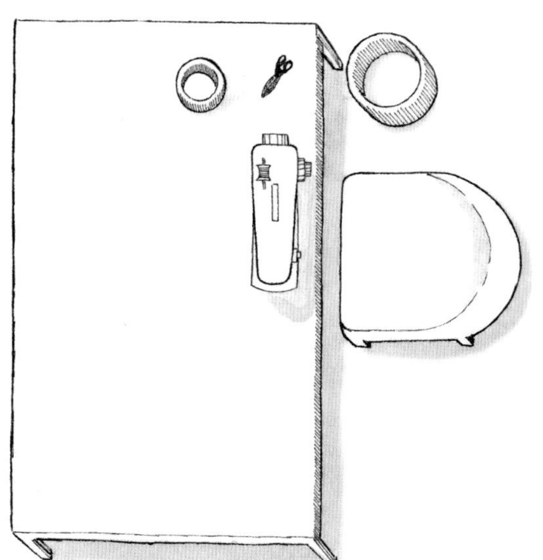

If this is the case, at least commandeer a shelf in a closet and keep all your supplies and machines together. Visibility is key—keep thread, notions, and tools in clear, plastic, labeled boxes. Store your prewashed (and labeled) fabric with matching thread, buttons, interfacing, and other related notions in clear, self-sealing plastic bags.

Your sewing table should be large enough to fit your sewing machine and your fabric and supplies. You'll also need a comfortable chair—preferably swivel—and adequate lighting. An extra gooseneck lamp directs task lighting where you need it. Set up an ironing board nearby your sewing table so you can use it frequently.

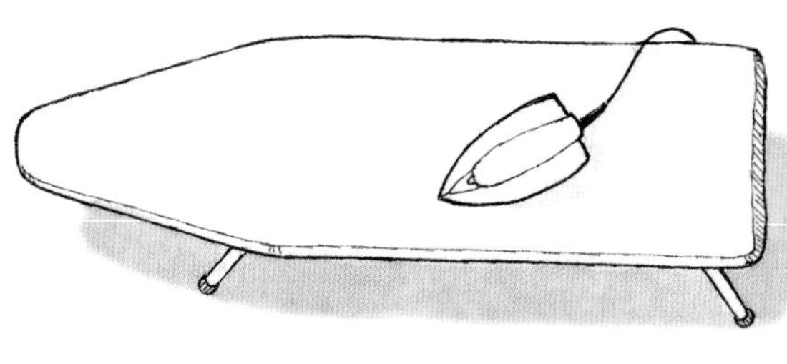

When you're not using your sewing machine, cover it to keep dust out. Most machines have a soft or hard cover. Or you can simply drape the machine with a cloth — or sew your own quick cover!

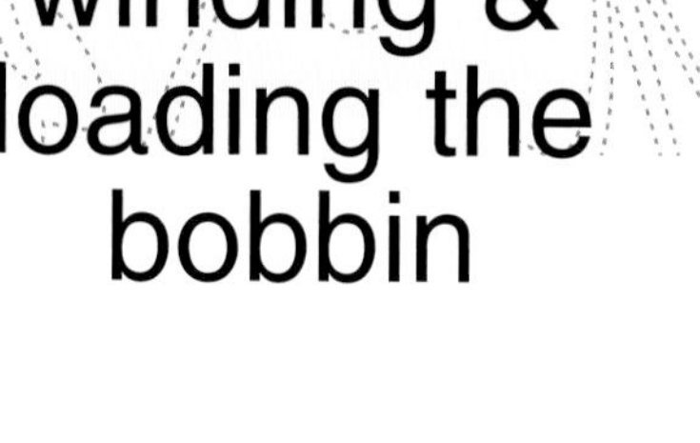

winding & loading the bobbin

The methods for winding thread onto a bobbin and for loading the bobbin into the machine are different for every machine—so check your owner's manual. Begin with an empty bobbin and wind at a constant, medium speed so the thread winds evenly. Do not overwind the bobbin.

wind on top: Most machines have a mechanism on top for bobbin winding. The machine is threaded specifically to wind the bobbin.

wind in place: Top-loading bobbins often wind in place with the machine threaded as if to sew. This system is convenient because you don't have to unthread the machine each time you need to refill the bobbin.

wind with separate motor: Some new machines feature a second motor for winding bobbins.

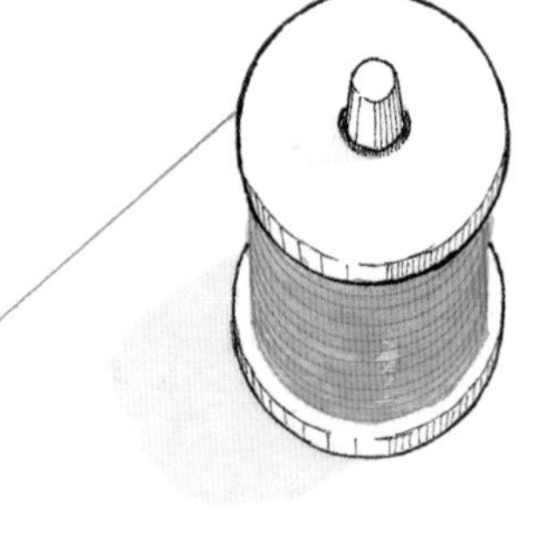

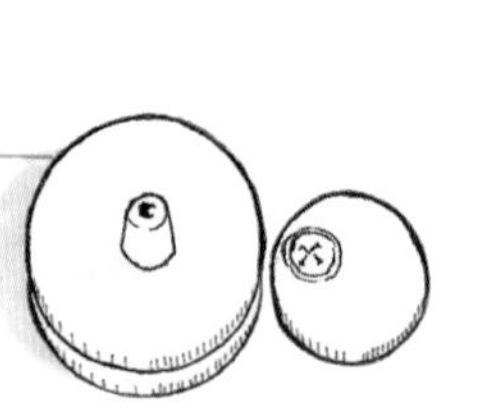

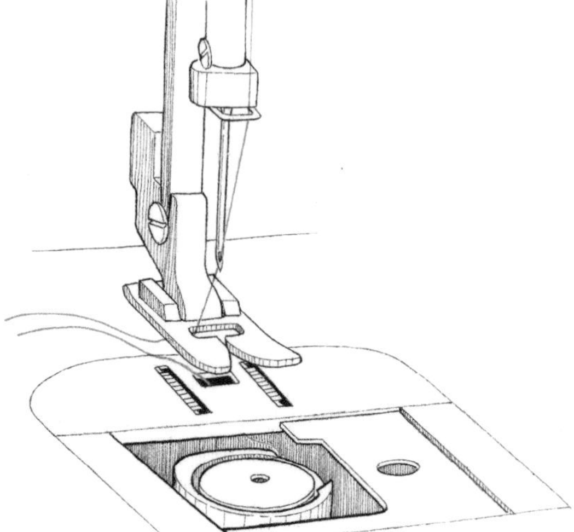

load at top: Drop the bobbin in the top of the machine bed and draw the thread through the tension guide.

load at front or side: Place the bobbin in the case and slide the thread under the bobbin-case tension spring. Place the bobbin case in the machine cavity.

drawing bobbin thread to top: Hold the needle thread while turning the balance wheel toward you one full rotation. As the needle goes down, the top thread interlocks with the bobbin thread and brings it up through the needle hole. Pull both threads together under the presser foot and off to the side or back.

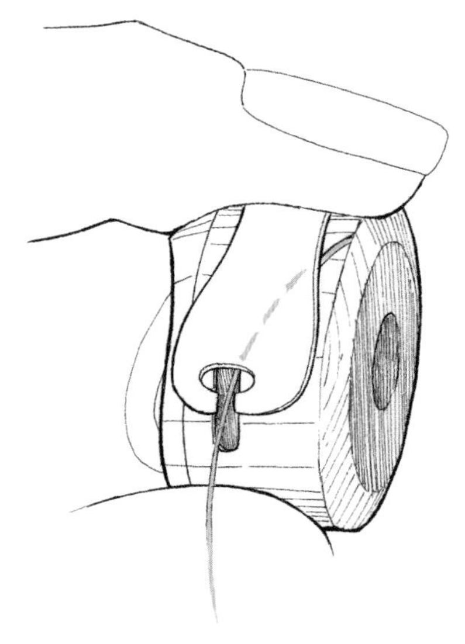

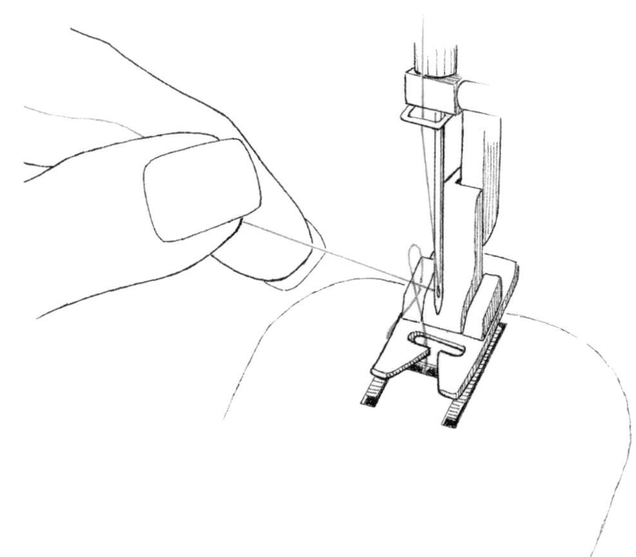

threading the sewing machine

To ensure a good stitch, you must thread the machine correctly. The thread path is usually marked somewhere on the machine. If the path is unclear, refer to the manual.

1. Insert a new needle. Loosen the needle clamp, slide the old needle out and the new one in, and tighten the clamp. Usually the flat side of the shank goes toward the back of the machine, and the groove in the needle shaft faces the front.

2. Wind the bobbin and install it (see pages 40 and 41).

3. Raise the presser foot to open the tension discs, and raise the needle to its highest position.

4. Place the spool on the spool pin, and pull the thread to the left through the first thread guide.

5. Continue to draw the thread through the guides and the tension discs, following the marked thread path or the instructions in your manual. Make sure you don't skip a thread guide or you will distort the tension.

6. Pass the thread through the eye of the needle.

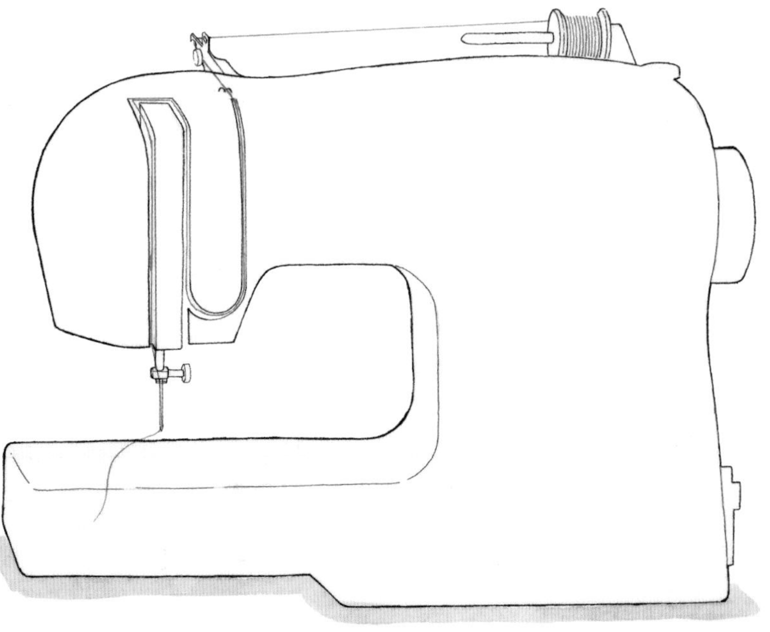

checking stitch tension

For a perfect, balanced stitch, the top and bobbin threads must interlock midway between the fabric layers. Only the needle thread should show on top of the fabric, and only the bobbin thread should show underneath. If the upper thread tension is too tight, the fabric may pucker. If it's too loose, unsightly loops may form on the underside.

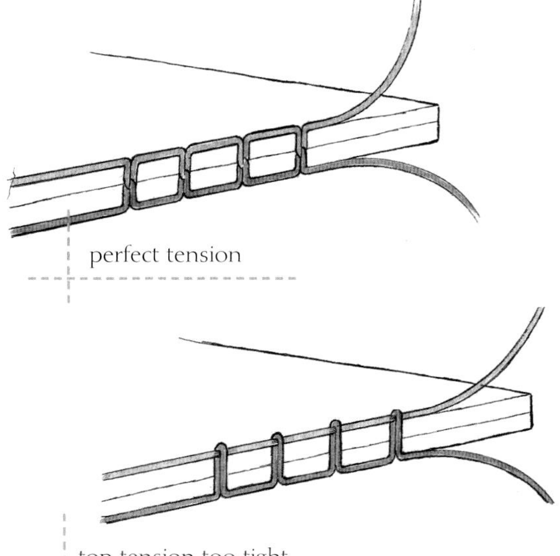

perfect tension

top tension too tight

To check your stitch tension, sew a seam with different colors of thread in the needle and bobbin. If both thread colors are visible on top, loosen the upper thread tension slightly. If you see both threads on the underside, tighten the tension slightly.

When manually adjusting the upper thread tension, make only a slight adjustment and then test it by sewing a seam on a scrap piece of your fabric. (The bobbin tension is factory-set and shouldn't be adjusted.)

As a general rule, loosen the tension for heavy fabrics and increase it for lightweight fabrics. Some machines have automatic tension control—the machine senses the fabric thickness and self-adjusts.

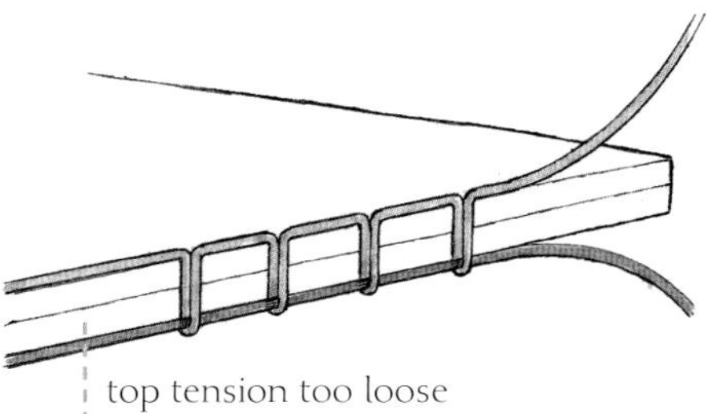

top tension too loose

If stitch tension is off. . .

- rethread the machine
- take out the bobbin and put it in again
- check that the needle isn't damaged
- adjust the upper thread tension slightly

prepare your fabric

Always preshrink your fabric before you lay it out and cut it—this way, you can be sure the finished garment or project won't shrink later. Preshrink the lining, zipper, and any trims, too. Launder everything in the same way you intend to launder the finished item. If you aren't sure the fabric is washable, cut a 6" (15.2 cm) square and launder it. After you remove it from the dryer, press and measure it. Is it still 6" (15.2 cm) square? Did it fade? Did it ravel excessively? If you are satisfied with the results, preshrink the entire yardage the same way.

If the fabric ravels, zigzag-stitch the cut edges before you launder it. Press the fabric as soon as it comes out of the dryer to eliminate wrinkles. Make sure to carefully press out the crease that formed when the fabric was wrapped on the bolt.

If the fabric can't be laundered, either steam the fabric to preshrink it or have it dry-cleaned. To steam-preshrink, first steam-press a small scrap of fabric to make sure the steam doesn't harm it. Then dampen the fabric or a press cloth and press the wrong side of the fabric until the water has evaporated. Shoot steam into the fibers as you press.

Before laying out your pattern, find the straight grain of the fabric and straighten the cut ends.

straightening fabric grain

Grain refers to the direction of the fabric threads. Lengthwise grain is parallel to the selvages. Crosswise grain is perpendicular to the selvage. Bias grain is diagonal, and the grain of the fabric with "true bias" runs 45 degrees to the lengthwise and crosswise grains.

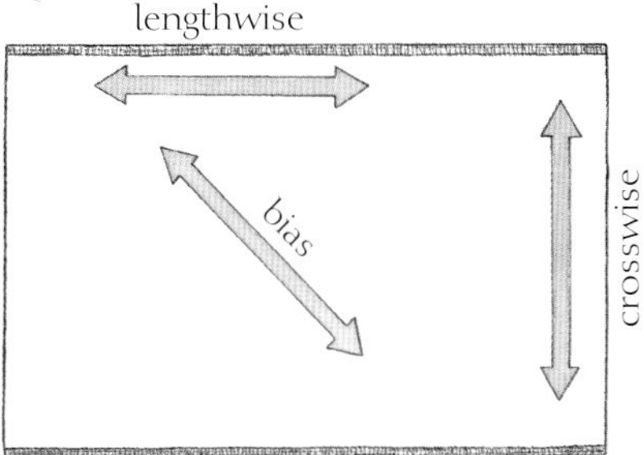

Most garments are cut so the lengthwise grain runs from the top of the garment to the hem (see page 46). This layout produces the most stable fabric pieces and the most economical use of the fabric. Garments made from border print fabrics are usually cut on the crosswise grain.

Bias-cut garments stretch in both directions, so they require special techniques for seaming and hemming (see pages 56, 88, and 90). They hang beautifully and tend to skim the body with a fluid elegance, so skirts and eveningwear are often cut on the bias.

Checking the Grain

Woven fabric must be "on-grain"—with lengthwise and crosswise yarns at right angles to each other—so garments hang smoothly and seams are straight. Here's how to check your fabric:

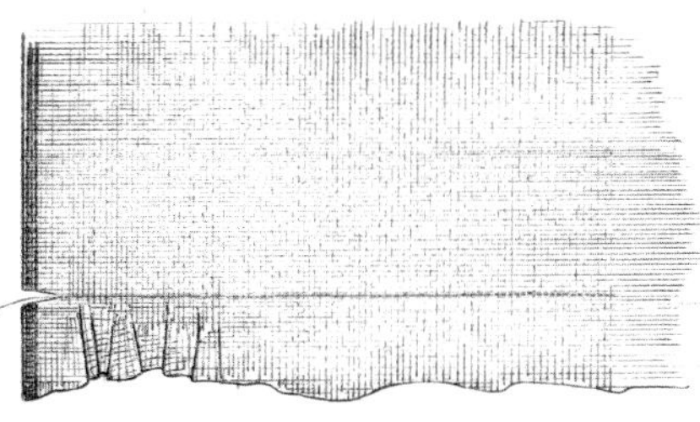

1. Snip into the selvage and pull a crosswise yarn so the fabric puckers. Cut along the puckered yarn to the opposite selvage. The cut creates a perfectly straight grainline in the crosswise direction.

2. Fold the fabric in half lengthwise, aligning the selvages, and smooth it flat. The cut ends should be even. If the ends don't align, shift the layers until they do. Pin the layers together along the selvages and ends at frequent intervals. Steam-press the fabric to align the fibers along the grainlines.

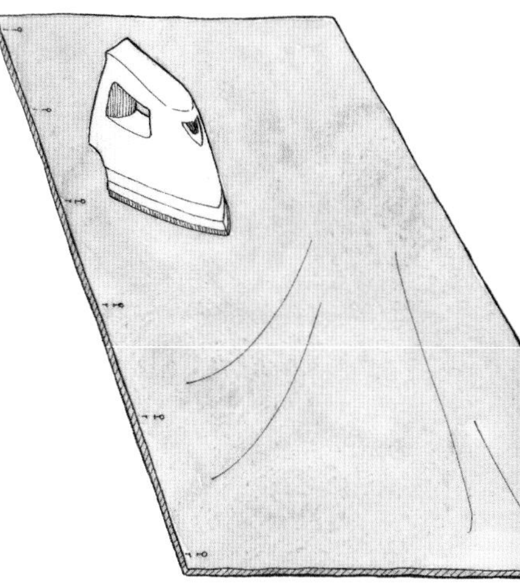

preparing & laying out the pattern

Check the pattern instruction sheet to determine which pattern pieces you need. Cut them apart, leaving extra pattern tissue beyond the cutting lines in case you need to lengthen or widen a piece. The extra tissue also makes it easier to cut the fabric. Press the pattern pieces with a warm, dry iron so they are flat. Make any necessary fitting adjustments (see page 37).

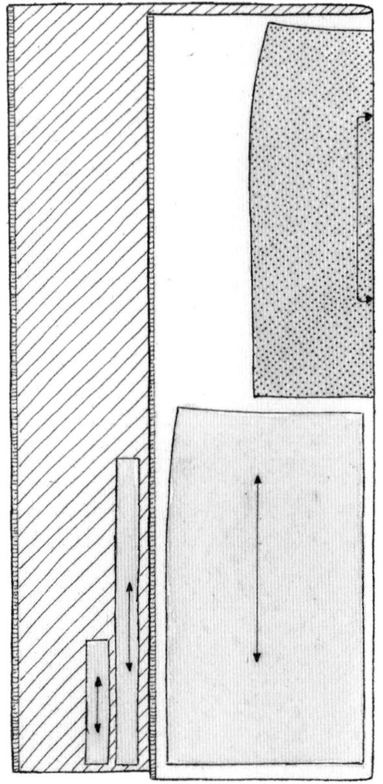

On your instruction sheet, circle or highlight the cutting layout for the fabric width, size, and view of the items you are making. Follow the "with nap" layout if the fabric is a directional print—has a definite up and down—or has a surface pile (see pages 96 and 97). Position all the pieces in the same direction, so the top of each piece is near the same end of the fabric.

Clear a large, flat surface so you can lay out the fabric so it is straight and smooth. If the fabric looks the same on both sides, choose and mark the wrong side with tailor's chalk or a fabric-marking pen. After you cut the pieces, make sure there's a mark on each piece.

Fold the fabric as the layout indicates (most often with selvages and right sides of the fabric together). Do not use the fabric selvage as a straight edge. Position the pieces away from the selvages to avoid puckered seams.

Arrange the pattern pieces on the folded fabric, following the layout guide and beginning with the largest pieces. If the pattern piece is shaded in the guide, place the piece with the printed side down. Place unshaded pieces face up. Leave room to cut any pieces that need more than two fabric pieces. Refer to the section on matching prints, plaids, stripes, and napped fabrics, if it applies (see pages 96 to 99).

pinning the pattern

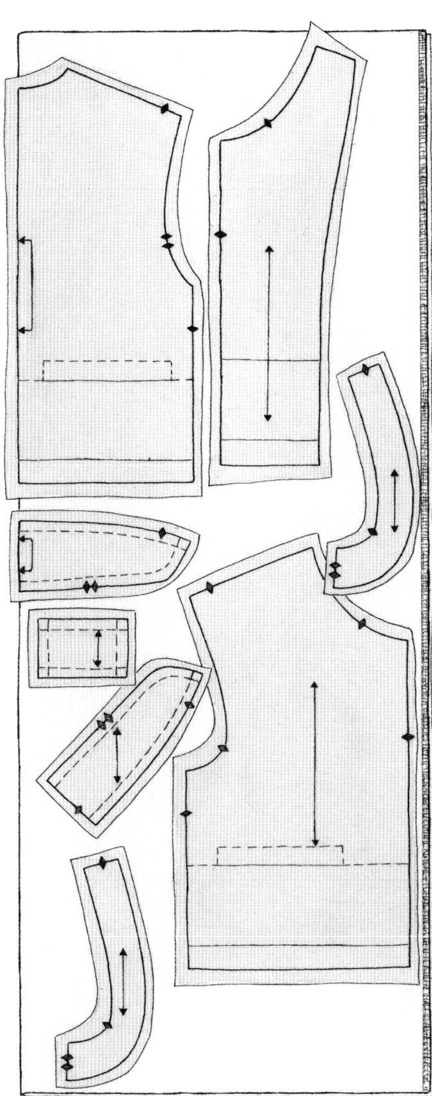

If you adjusted the pattern tissue and the pieces don't fit on the fabric, overlap the tissue pieces—but only outside the cutting lines. If the pieces still don't fit on the fabric, consider shortening the garment slightly at the hem.

Pin all pieces before cutting. To make sure all the pieces are straight, pin the pieces along the fold first. Then pin the largest of the remaining pattern pieces. Put a pin at the center of the grainline. Measure from the edge of the fabric to each end of the grainline to make sure the piece is straight, as shown in the drawing below.

Pin the corners and then the edges, smoothing the pattern as you work. Place the pins within the seam allowance, diagonal to the corners and perpendicular to the edges, with points toward the cutting lines. Space pins about 3" (7.6 cm) apart (but slightly closer together on slippery fabrics and curved cutting lines). Fill in the unused areas of fabric with the smaller pattern pieces. Pin them as you did the larger pieces.

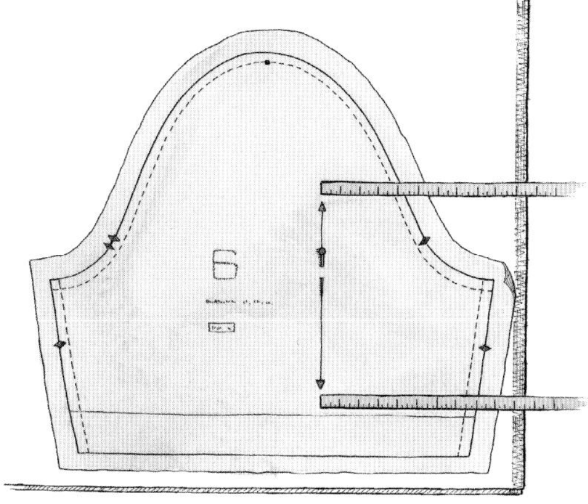

If the entire length of fabric doesn't fit on your cutting surface, pin the pattern pieces at just one end. Fold the fabric, with the pieces inside, and pin the remaining pattern pieces onto the next section of fabric.

cutting the fabric

Double-check that the pattern pieces are positioned correctly and pinned securely before you begin to cut. Place one hand on the table, close to the cutting line to hold the fabric flat. Work with a sharp, dressmaker's shears (page 15)—the bent handle helps keep the fabric flat. Hold your shears to the right of the cutting line for greatest accuracy. Cut with long, firm strokes on straight edges and with shorter ones around curves.

Cut notches outward, if that is how they are drawn. Or you can make short snips into the seam allowance at the notch location. To snip, cut 1/8" (3 mm) into the seam allowance with only the tips of the scissors, taking care not to cut through the seam line. Snips are a perfect way to mark notches, the ends of darts, fold lines, and the center front and back.

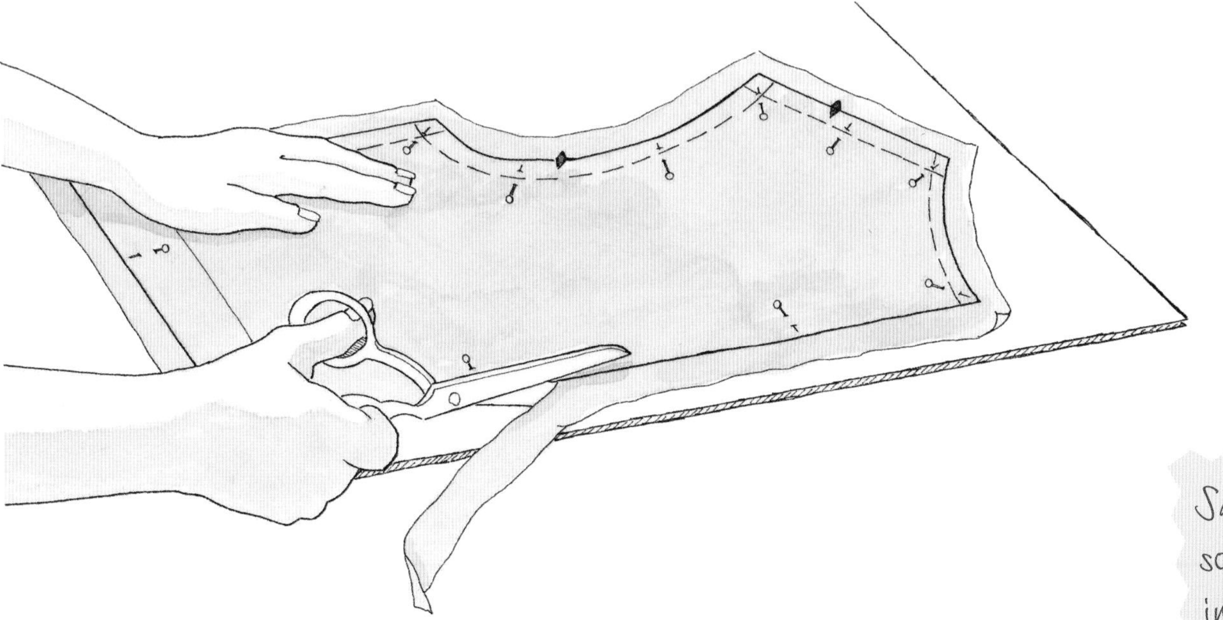

Save your fabric scraps so you can later test interfacing weight, stitch quality, pressing, and buttonholes.

marking the fabric

Transfer key markings from the pattern to the fabric after cutting and before removing the tissue.

You should always test any type of marking tool (except thread basting) on a scrap piece of your fabric. For a description of the various types of marking tools, see page 16. The markings are temporary so you should be able to remove them easily, but make sure they stay on for as long as you need to refer to them. Chalk rubs off easily, and air-soluble marking pens disappear in 24 to 48 hours, so mark close to sewing time.

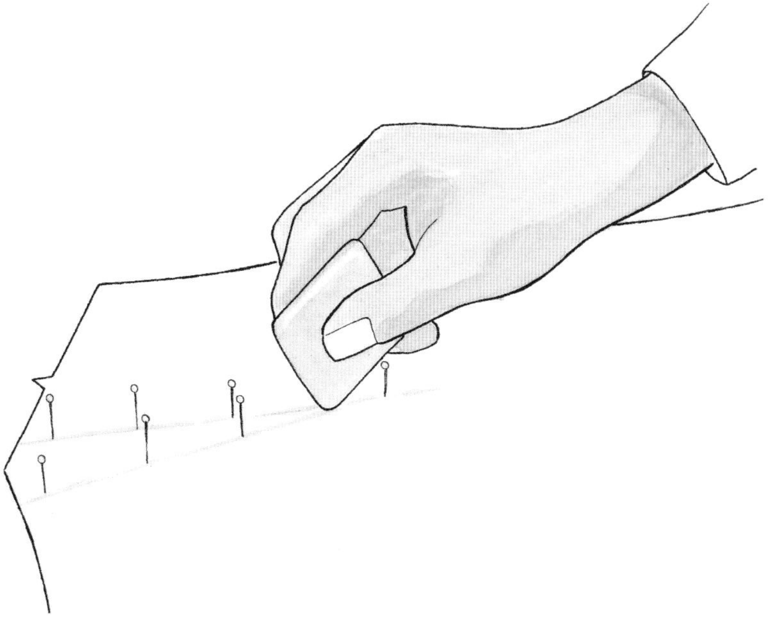

Transfer darts, tucks, gathering and pleat lines, buttonholes, and pocket or other placement lines. If the marks are more helpful on the right side of the fabric (for example, the placement of patch pockets), transfer them with a marking pen or tracing wheel to the wrong side. Then hand-baste over the marks to mark the right side with thread.

chalk and fabric-marking pens: To mark with chalk and fabric marking pens, first place pins at the symbols through the pattern and fabric layers. Carefully pull the pattern away from the fabric and over the pins. Mark the pin location on the top layer of the fabric with the chalk or marking pen. Turn the fabric over and mark the same pin locations on that side. Remove the pins, separate the layers, and connect the markings (if necessary—for example, for darts).

tracing wheel and tracing paper: To mark with a tracing wheel and tracing paper, insert two pieces of dressmaker's tracing paper so the carbon or wax side of the paper faces the wrong side of each fabric layer. Roll the tracing wheel over the mark. Use a ruler as a guide when marking long straight lines. Mark dots, notches, or other small symbols with short lines or Xs. Remove the pattern tissue and tracing paper.

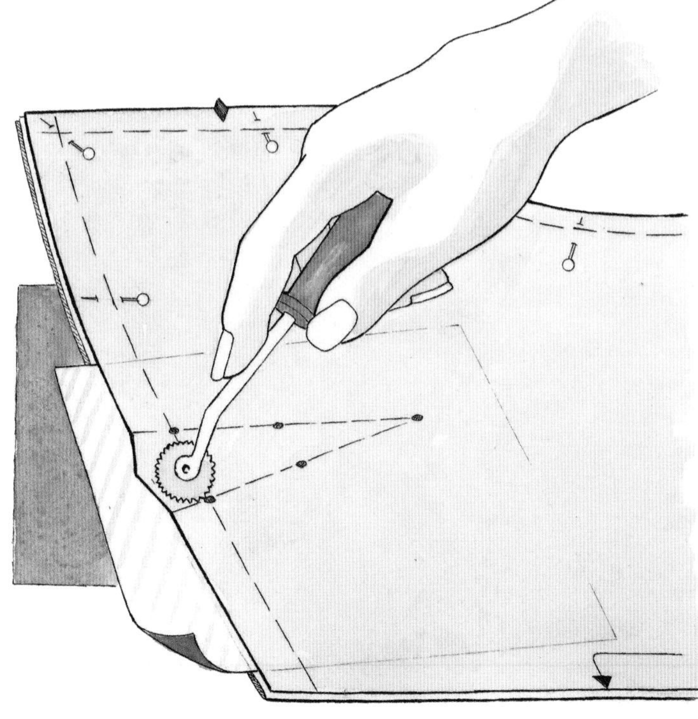

snips, basting, and tacks: You can mark notches, dots, center back and center front markings with snips into the seam allowance.

You can also mark construction elements by hand-basting with thread. Thread a needle with a single, unknotted strand. Take long running stitches to mark straight lines. Leave long thread tails.

You can mark pattern symbols with thread tacks. With double, unknotted thread, insert the needle in and out of the symbol, through pattern and both layers of fabric. Cut the thread, leaving 1" (2.5 cm) tails. Carefully remove the pattern, slightly separate the fabric layers, and clip the thread, leaving thread tufts on each layer.

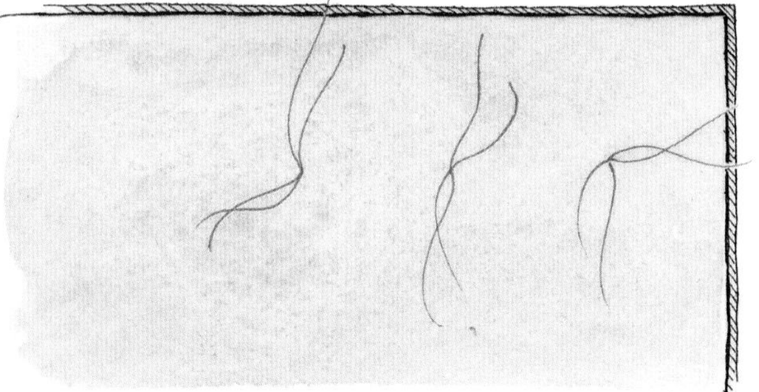

check before you sew

- [ ] Organize your sewing area. Position the sewing machine on the right side of your worktable so the bulk of the fabric can rest on the left side. Keep a wastebasket nearby or tape a small trash bag to the edge of the worktable to catch thread snips and fabric scraps.
- [ ] Throughout your work area, provide adequate overhead lighting and task lighting for close-up work.
- [ ] Set up an iron and ironing board. Keep a press cloth handy, too (a scrap of muslin works well).
- [ ] Gather all the necessary sewing tools and notions before you start your project. Keep sewing scissors, pins, a pincushion, and a seam ripper within reach.
- [ ] Prepare and preshrink your fabric. Press out the center crease and make sure the fabric grain line is straight (see page 45).
- [ ] Read the pattern instruction sheet from beginning to end.
- [ ] Cut out the necessary pattern pieces and press out any wrinkles with a warm, dry iron.
- [ ] Put a new needle in the machine (the rule of thumb is: a new needle after every eight hours of use).
- [ ] Fill a bobbin with the same thread that is on the thread spool.
- [ ] Brush the bobbin area and feed dogs to remove lint (most machines come with a small lint brush).
- [ ] Raise the presser foot and thread the machine, referring to your machine manual for accuracy.
- [ ] Practice stitching on a scrap of your fabric. Notice the length and tension of the machine stitches. Make any necessary adjustments.
- [ ] Take a deep breath, relax, and begin—but, most important, have fun!

construction stitches

Most sewing machines have a variety of built-in stitches, but you can accomplish anything with just a simple straight stitch. Straight stitches form the basis for several construction techniques, each with its own purpose and finished effect.

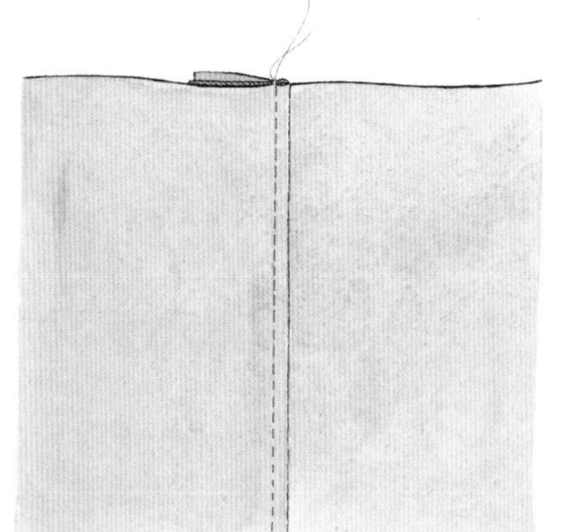

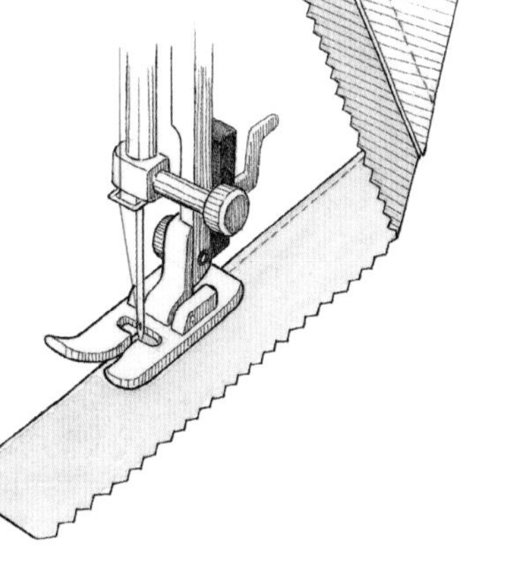

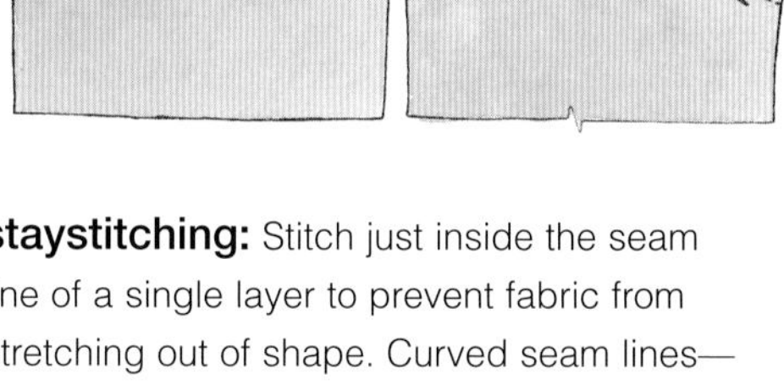

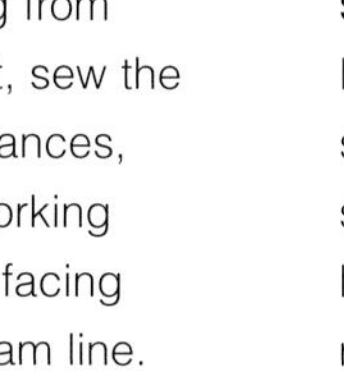

edgestitching: Stitch close to the seam line or edge to make a seam lie flat, as shown above. To create a sharp crease, stitch along a fold very close to the edge. Stitch from the bottom toward the top of a garment.

understitching: To prevent a facing from rolling to the right side of the garment, sew the seam, trim and grade the seam allowances, and press them toward the facing. Working from the right side, stitch through the facing and seam allowances close to the seam line.

staystitching: Stitch just inside the seam line of a single layer to prevent fabric from stretching out of shape. Curved seam lines—such as necklines, facings, armholes, waistlines, and side seams over the hip area—require staystitching.

To turn a corner, leave the needle in the fabric, lift the presser foot, and turn the fabric. Lower the presser foot and continue stitching.

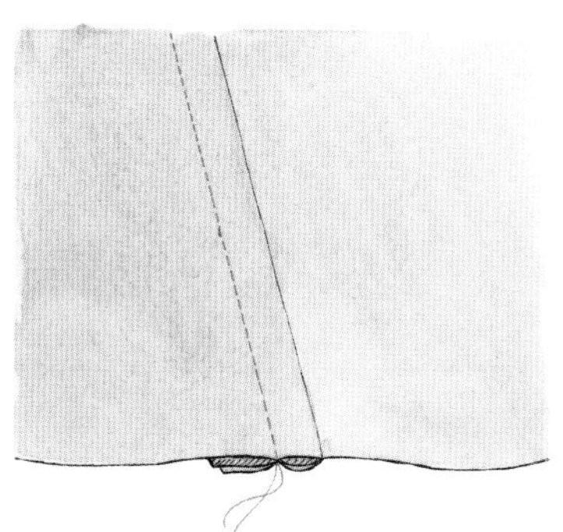

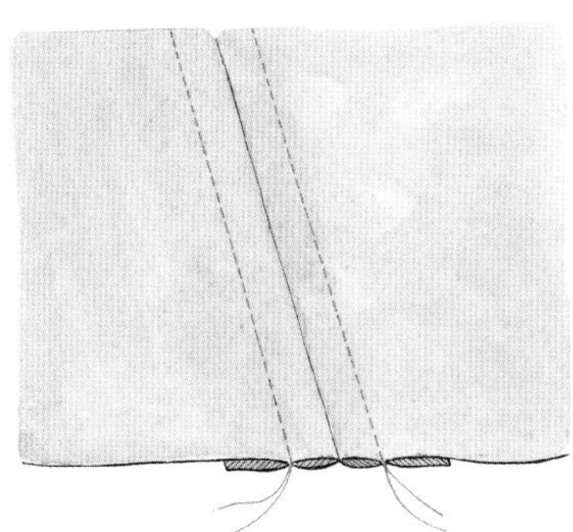

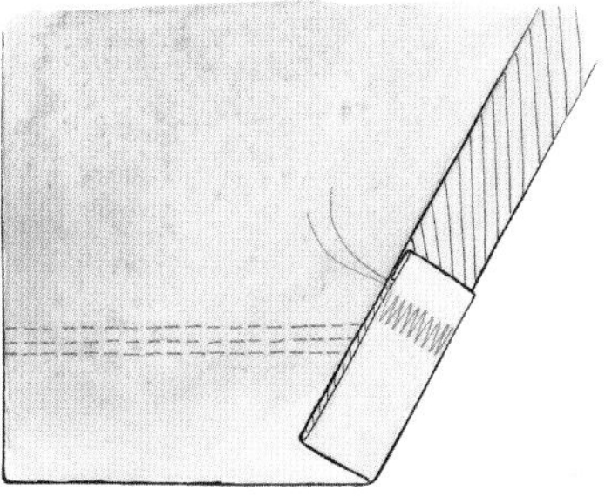

topstitching: Straight stitches are stitched on the right side of the fabric to emphasize a detail, to hold seam allowances in place, and/or to create design interest. Work with topstitching thread and a stitch length of 6 to 8 stitches per inch (2.5 cm).

single topstitched seam: Press both seam allowances toward one side of the seam. Stitch through all the layers 1⁄4" to 3⁄8" (6 mm to 1 cm) from the seam, catching the seam allowances underneath.

double topstitched seam: Press open the seam allowances. Topstitch 1⁄4" to 3⁄8" (6 mm to 1 cm) from the seam line on each side, catching the seam allowances underneath. Stitch both sides in the same direction—from the bottom toward the top.

multiple rows of topstitching: Work with a twin or triple needle for perfectly parallel topstitching rows (see page 8). The stitches will have some give, so this method is useful for knits and stretch woven fabrics.

the perfect seam

Seams are the basic construction elements that hold fabric pieces together. Most often, you will sew a straight-stitch seam with a stitch length of 8 to 12 stitches per inch (2.5 cm). If the fabric is heavy, set the machine for a longer stitch length—6 to 10 stitches per inch (2.5 cm). If the fabric is lightweight, set the stitch length to a shorter length—about 12 to 14 stitches per inch (2.5 cm). The seam allowance is 5⁄8" (1.6 cm) unless otherwise noted on the pattern tissue and instruction sheet.

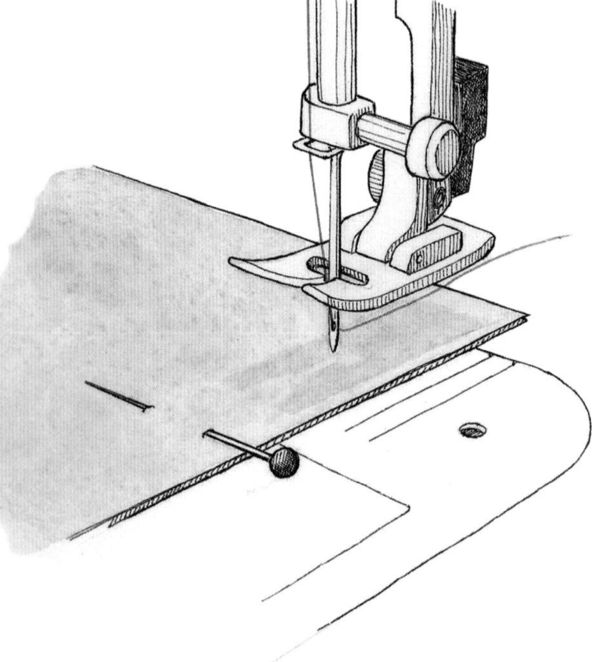

Test the stitch on a scrap piece of your fabric before you begin sewing. You may need to adjust the presser-foot pressure and the stitch tension if you are sewing different fabric thicknesses. If the stitches look too tight, loose, or uneven, rethread the machine—nine times out of ten rethreading will fix the problem.

1. Pin the fabric layers with right sides together (unless otherwise noted) and raw edges even. Insert pins perpendicular to the edge about every 2" (5.1 cm), with all the heads facing in the same direction so you can remove them easily as you come to them.
2. Lift the presser foot and raise the needle to its highest position by turning the handwheel toward you.
3. Position the fabric under the presser foot so the cut edges align with the 5⁄8" (1.6 cm) seam allowance marking on the throat plate and the top edges are slightly behind the presser foot.
4. Lower the presser foot. Adjust the machine setting to stitch in reverse. Backstitch to the top edges of the fabric, holding the thread tails for the first few stitches.
5. Change the machine setting to stitch forward. Stitch over the backstitches and continue stitching to the end of the seam.
6. Backstitch again for about 1⁄2" (1.3 cm). Raise the presser foot and pull the fabric out from under it. If the bobbin thread does not release easily, turn the handwheel toward you slightly. Clip the threads close to the stitching.

To avoid tangles, hold the bobbin and top threads to the back or side until you take the first few stitches.

trimming a seam

Pressing is often enough to make seams lie flat—but sometimes you need to trim the seam allowances to reduce bulk. Trimming also helps smooth curves and sharpen corners.

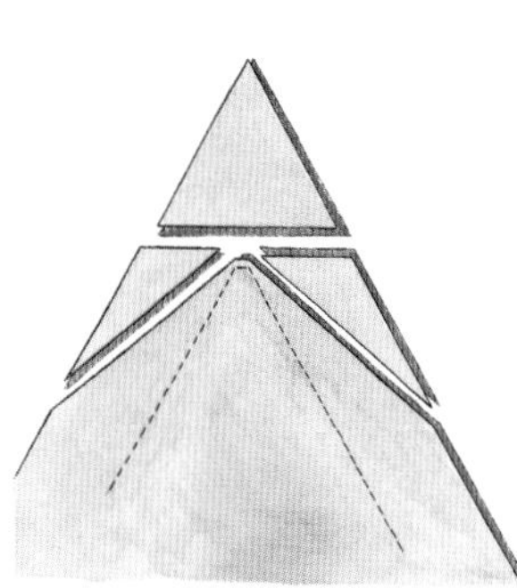

trimming a point: Trim the seam allowances straight across the point first. Then taper the allowances along each side.

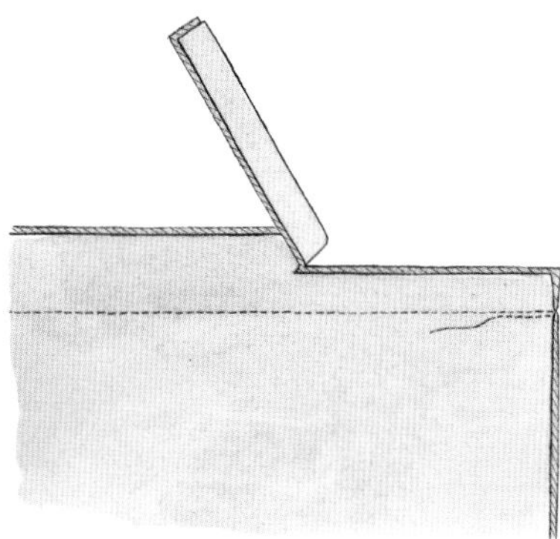

trimming: Cut away half of the seam allowance width.

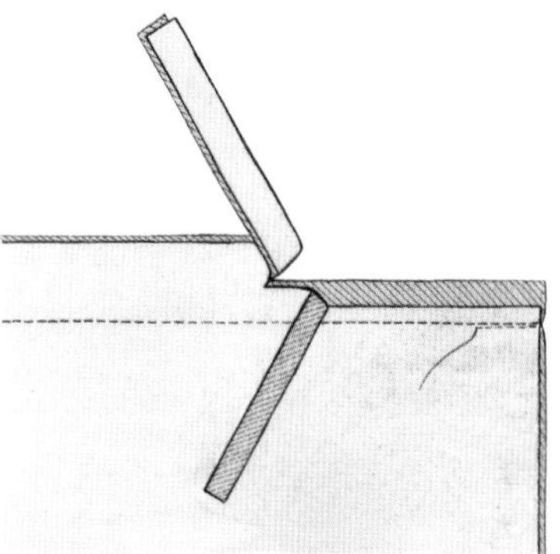

grading: Grade enclosed seams (waist-bands) and garment edges (lapel, front opening) to eliminate a thick ridge. After trimming both seam allowances, trim the seam allowance that will lie nearest the inside of the garment again, by about half its width.

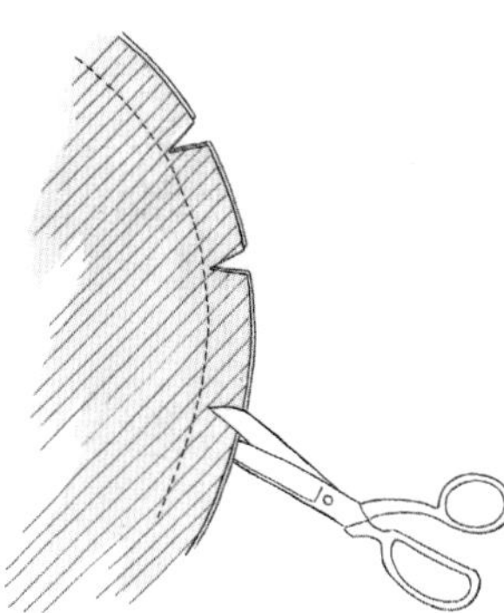

notching: Cut wedges out of the seam allow-ances of outward curves to remove extra fullness.

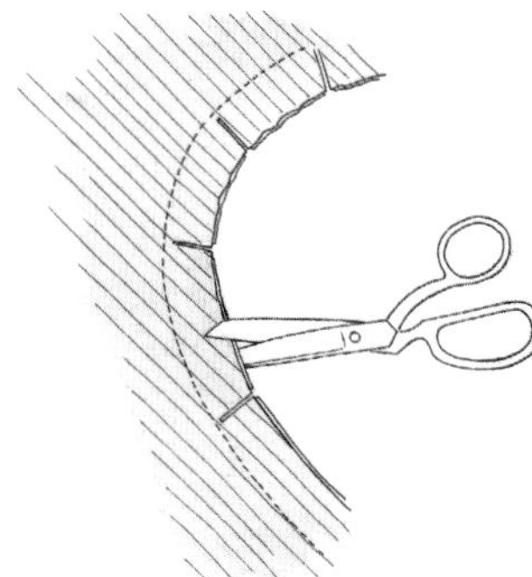

clipping: Cut short snips into the seam allowance of inward curves—working with only the tips of the scissors—to help them lie flat. Cut up to, but not through, the stitching.

types of seams

There are many types of seams you can use to join two pieces of fabric. Your choice depends on the fabric characteristics, the construction requirements, and the finished effect you would like to achieve.

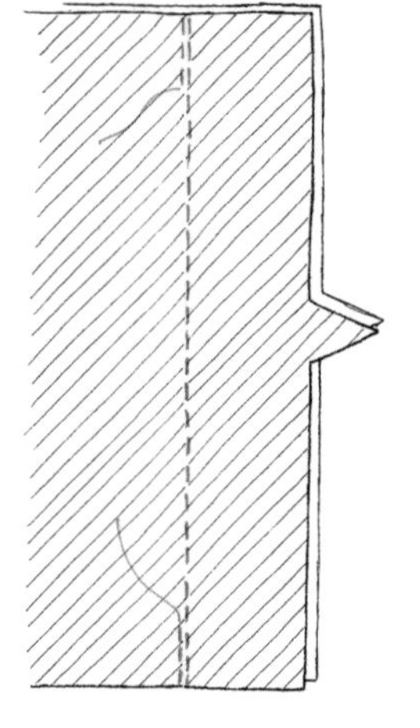

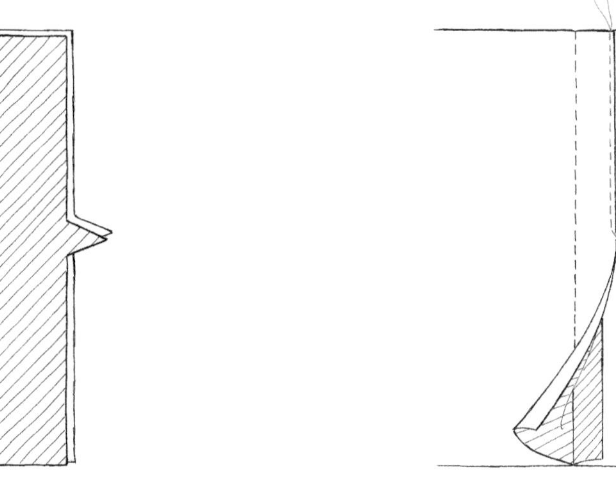

plain seam: This is the type of seam you'll use most often. With right sides together, stitch 5⁄8" (1.6 cm) from the edge. Backstitch two or three stitches at the beginning and end of the seam. Press the seam flat and then press it open.

narrow zigzag: This stitch prevents puckers by building stretch into the seam. It is effective with loose weaves and stretch fabrics. Set the machine for a narrow zigzag stitch and sew as you would a plain seam.

flat-fell seam: This style of seam adds strength to the construction. With wrong sides together, sew a 3⁄4" (1.9 cm) seam. Press the seam allowances to one side. Trim the lower seam allowance to 1⁄8" (3 mm). Press under 1⁄4" (6 mm) of the upper seam allowance, and pin it down, concealing the trimmed edge. Edgestitch on the fold (see page 52).

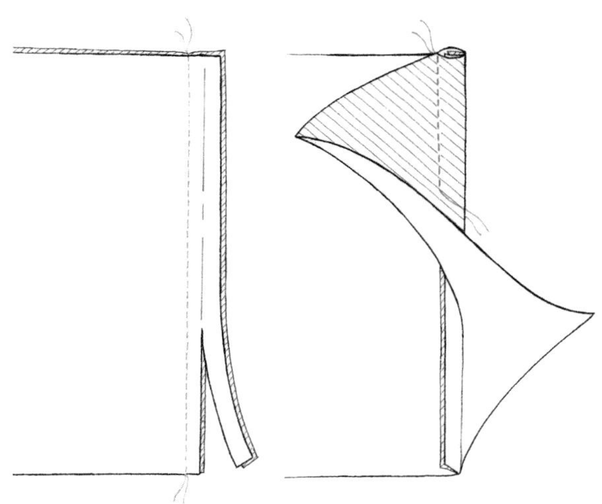

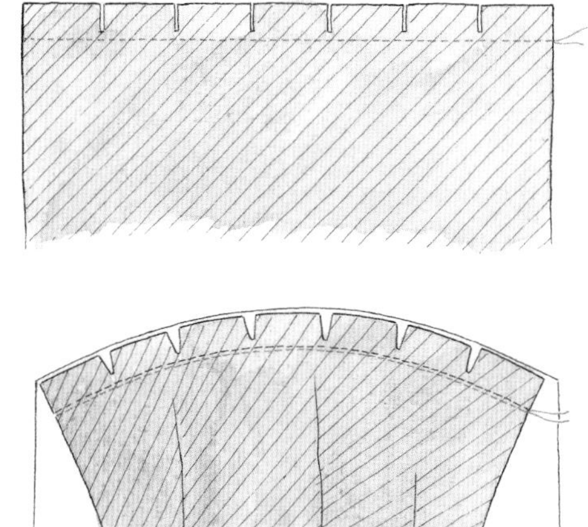

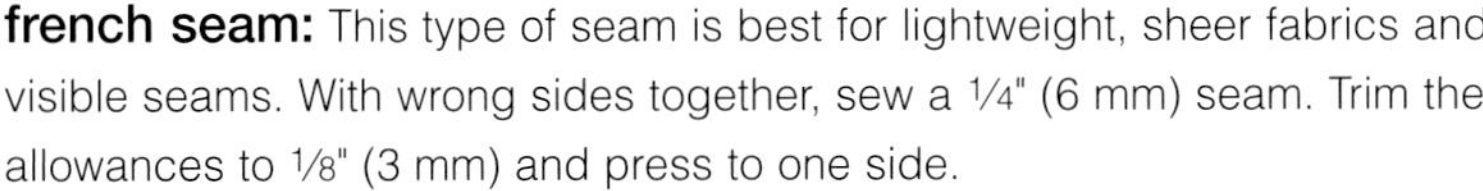

french seam: This type of seam is best for lightweight, sheer fabrics and visible seams. With wrong sides together, sew a 1⁄4" (6 mm) seam. Trim the allowances to 1⁄8" (3 mm) and press to one side.

Fold the right sides together (enclosing the trimmed seam), with the stitching line on the fold. Stitch 1⁄4" (6 mm) from the folded edge. Press the seam to one side.

seaming a straight edge and a curve: Staystitch just inside the seam line of the straight edge (see page 52). Clip into the seam allowance up to, but not through, the stitching. Pin the pieces right sides together, with the clipped edge on top, matching any marks. Clips will spread so the edges match. Stitch, with the clipped edge on top, keeping the bottom layer flat. Press the seam open on a tailor's ham (see page 18).

To keep seams from shifting, pin or hand-baste — or use a walking (even-feed) presser foot (page 10).

seam finishes

For a neat and professional finish, you should finish all your seams—unless the garment is lined. Finished seams also add durability to garments you will launder regularly. French and flat-fell seams (pages 56 and 57) enclose the raw edges, so they don't require further finishing.

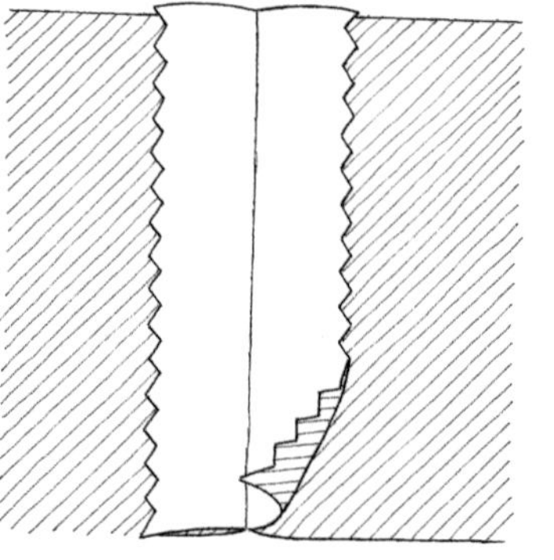

pinked edge: Working with pinking shears, cut a sawtooth edge along each seam allowance. A pinked edge is the simplest type of seam finish, although it does not entirely eliminate raveling.

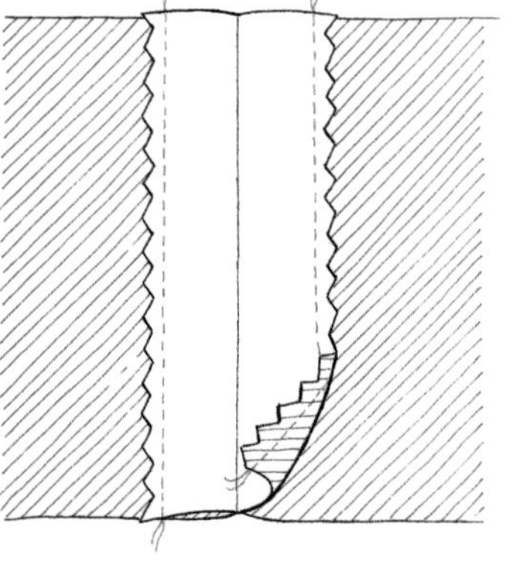

stitch and pink: Press the seam open and stitch 1/4" (6 mm) from the edge of each seam allowance. Cut the edge with pinking shears. This finish is more effective than pinking alone.

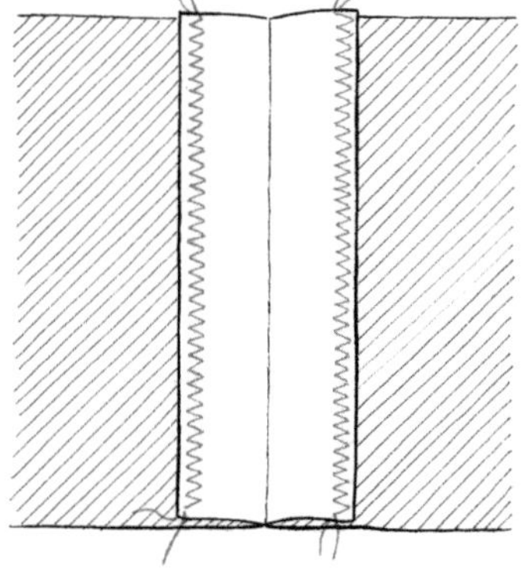

zigzag: Press the seam open. Set the machine to stitch a wide, medium-length zigzag. Stitch along the edge of each seam allowance so the stitches abut the raw edge to prevent raveling. For lightweight fabrics, zigzag the seam allowances together and press to one side.

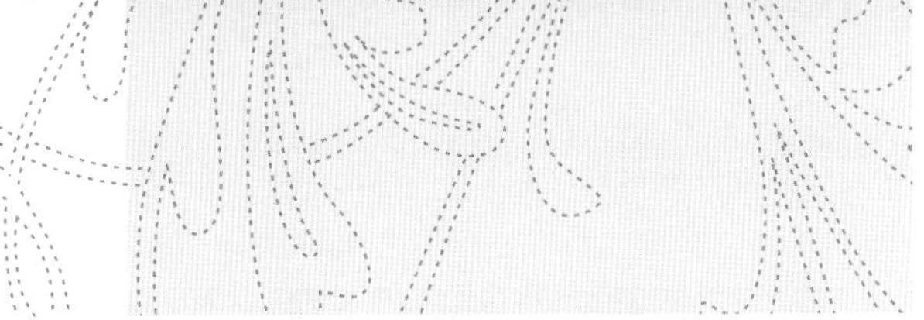

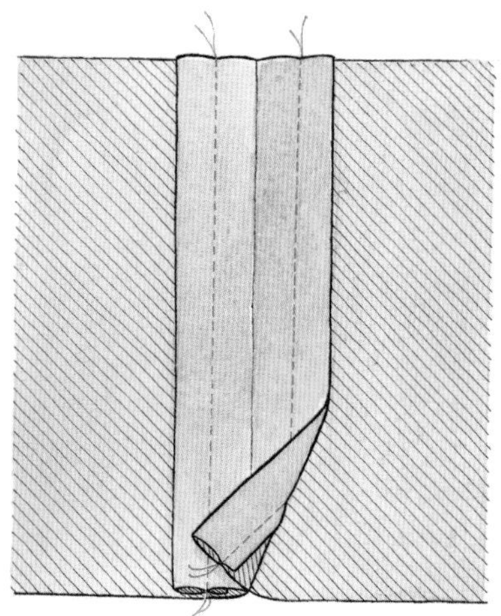

turn and stitch: Turn under each seam allowance edge 1/8" to 1/4" (3 to 6 mm), and press. Stitch through the seam allowance to catch the folded edge.

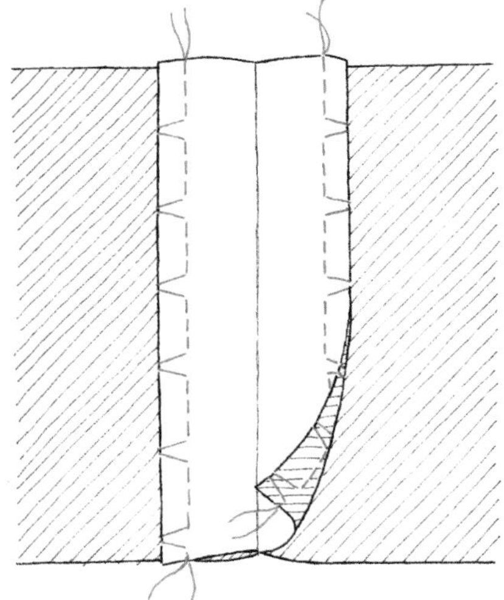

machine overedge: Press open the seam and set your machine to a built-in stitch that combines straight and zigzag stitches. Stitch along the edges of the seam allowances.

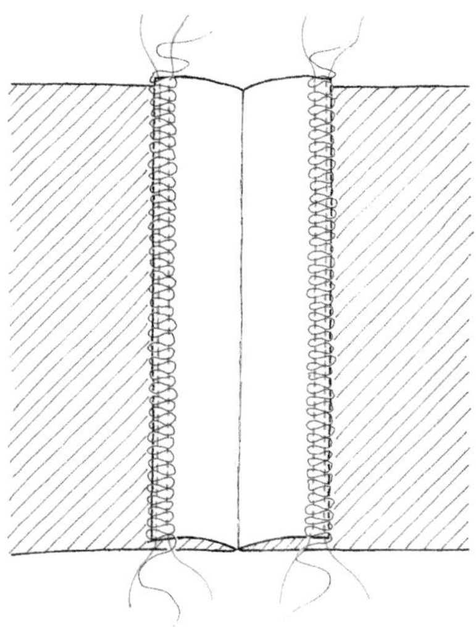

overlock: Any two-, three-, or four-thread overlock stitch, made with a serger (or overlock machine, see page 12), produces a professional-looking finish.

hand stitches

Hand sewing is sometimes quicker and more efficient than machine sewing—when you need to carefully match surface patterns, when the work area is small and tight, or when you don't want visible stitches on the right side. To stitch by hand, thread a hand needle with 18" (45.7 cm) of thread and knot one end—or secure the end with one or two backstitches. For all stitches but the running stitch, pull the entire length of thread though the fabric with each stitch.

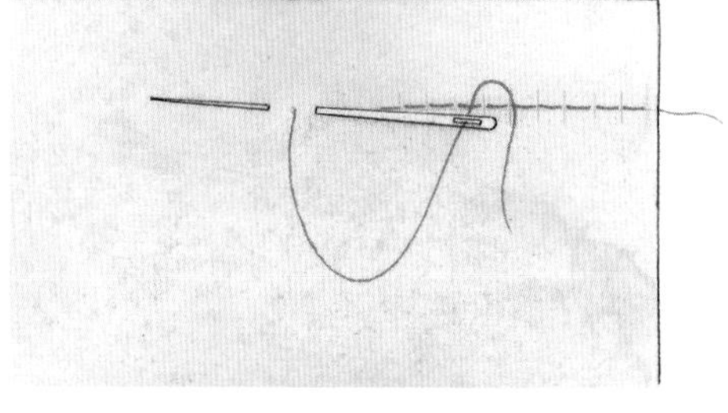

backstitch: This very strong stitch is used for seams. Bring the needle and thread to the right side of the fabric. Insert the needle 1/16" to 1/8" (1.6 to 3 mm) behind the point where the thread exited the fabric. Then bring the needle out through the fabric that same distance in front of that point. Repeat, inserting the needle into the previous exit point for each stitch.

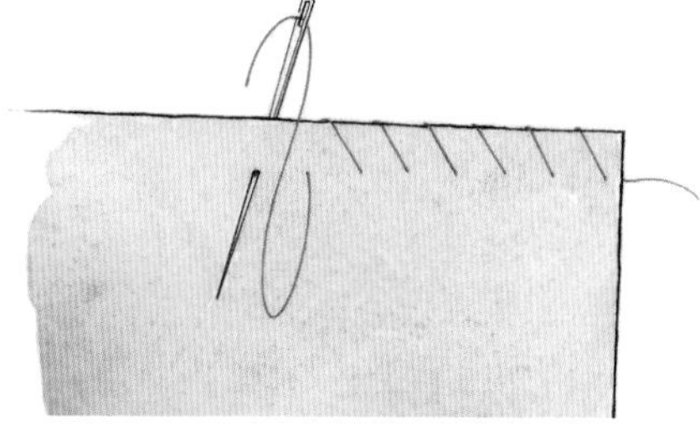

overcast stitch: This stitch is well suited for finishing edges. Form a series of close, evenly spaced, diagonal stitches 1/4" (6 mm) deep by passing the thread over and around the fabric edge.

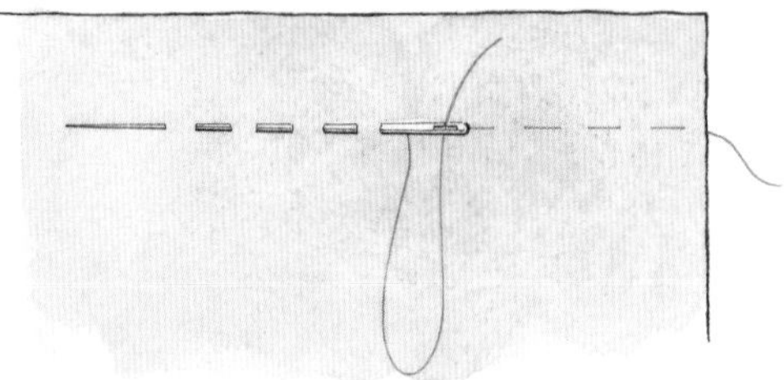

running stitch: This stitch is used for seams. Insert the point of the needle in and out of the fabric several times before pulling the thread through, thus completing several stitches at a time. Keep the stitches and spaces between them small and even.

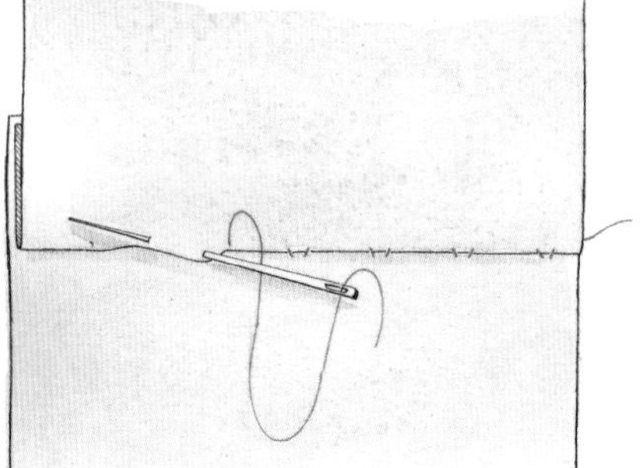

slip stitch: This stitch is handy for hemming, closing openings, and joining two folded edges. When joining folded edges, insert the needle inside the fabric fold and bring it out through the folded edge. Insert the needle into the fold of the opposite edge and bring it out through the fold about 1/4" (6 mm) away. Repeat, alternating from edge to edge with each stitch. When hemming or closing openings, alternate stitches from one fabric surface to the other.

basting methods

Basting is a reliable way to hold fabric layers or fabric and trim together temporarily. Basting is especially helpful when working with slippery fabrics, matching plaids, and applying trims. Baste with thread of a contrasting color to make it easier to see the stitches when it's time to remove them.

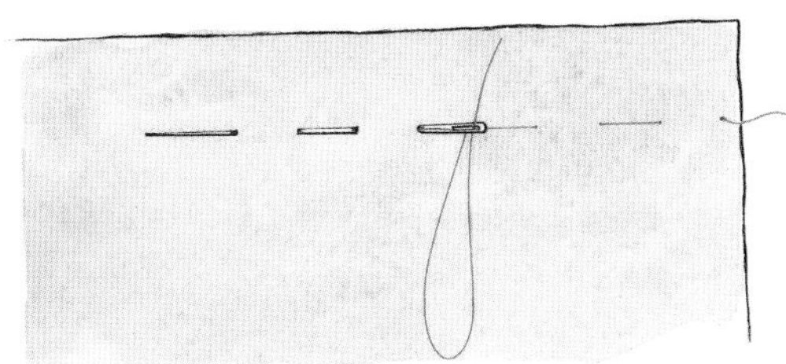

hand basting: This technique requires a long running stitch. Insert the needle in and out of the surface of the fabric to make several evenly spaced, 1⁄2" (1.3 cm) stitches. Pull the needle and thread through and repeat.

machine basting: This technique is effective when gathering. Adjust the machine-stitch length to the longest straight stitch, 3 to 6 stitches per inch (2.5 cm).

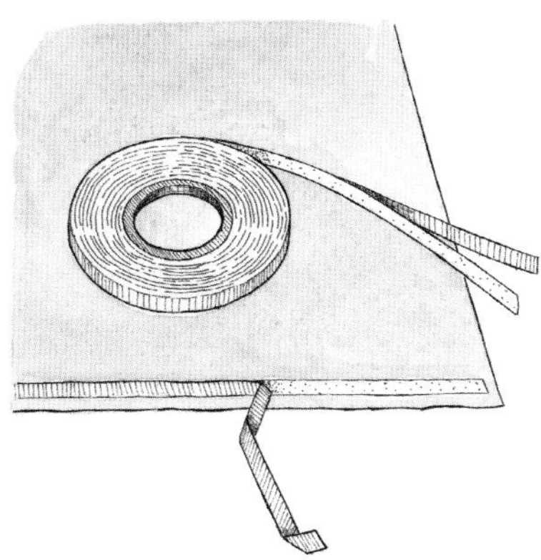

basting tape: This very narrow tape has adhesive on both sides with removable paper backing. Simply position the tape and press it in place with your fingers. Avoid stitching through it, as it will gum up your needle.

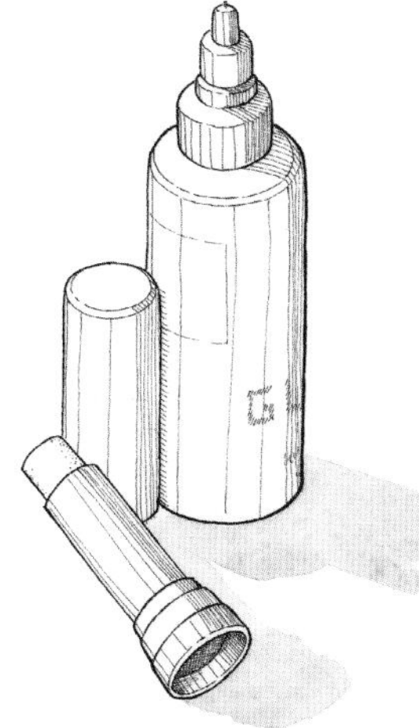

fabric glue: A glue stick or water-soluble glue, packaged in a tube applicator, temporarily holds fabric layers together to make it easier to sew the permanent stitches precisely.

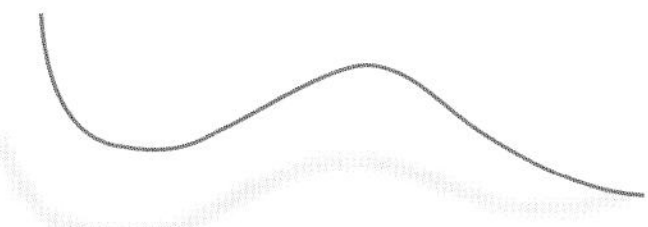

sewing darts

A dart adds dimension and shape to a flat piece of fabric, allowing the piece to mold to the body at the bust, waist, hips, or elbows. Different styles of darts are positioned in different areas of the garment, depending on the shaping needed. The single-pointed waist dart is the most common style.

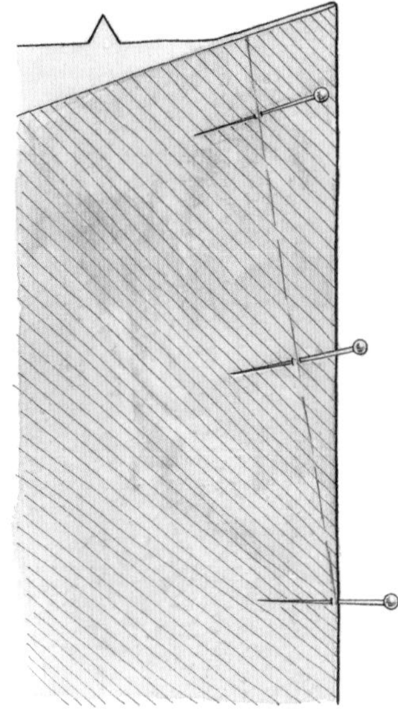

1. Mark a single-pointed dart using the pattern as a guide (see pages 49 and 50). Fold the dart down the center, right sides together, matching the stitching lines. Pin.

2. Begin stitching at the wide end, backstitching at the start. Continue stitching toward the point, removing pins as you stitch.

3. Taper your stitching so the last two or three stitches are directly on the fold. Do not backstitch at the point. Leave long thread tails.

4. Press the dart flat up to the point. Then, working with a tailor's ham, press the dart to one side (as indicated in the pattern instructions). Do not press over the point.

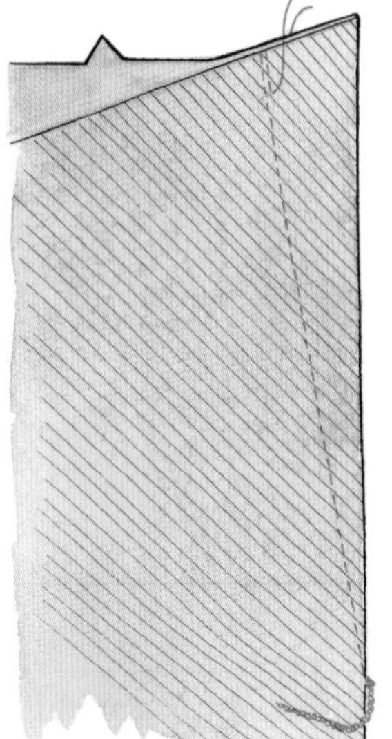

mitering corners & trims

Mitering is a method of minimizing bulk—for example, in the corners of patch pockets or on lengths of applied trim or ribbon. The two edges of fabric are joined diagonally to create a neat, flat miter.

Mitering Corners of Patch Pockets

1. Press all seam allowances to the inside of the pocket. Open the seam allowances and fold the corner diagonally so the crease marks line up at the seam line. Press the diagonal fold.

2. Open the fabric and refold, right sides together, bringing together the crease marks in the corner seam allowance. Stitch along the pressed diagonal fold.

3. Trim the corner seam allowance to 3⁄8" (1 cm) and press open.

4. Turn the seam allowances to the inside and press, forming a flat, mitered corner.

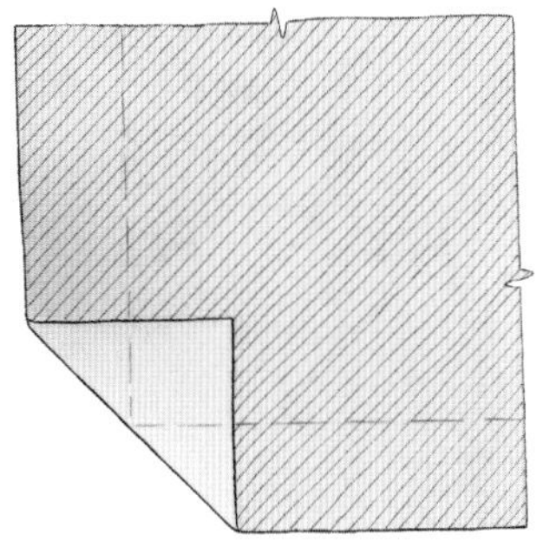

1

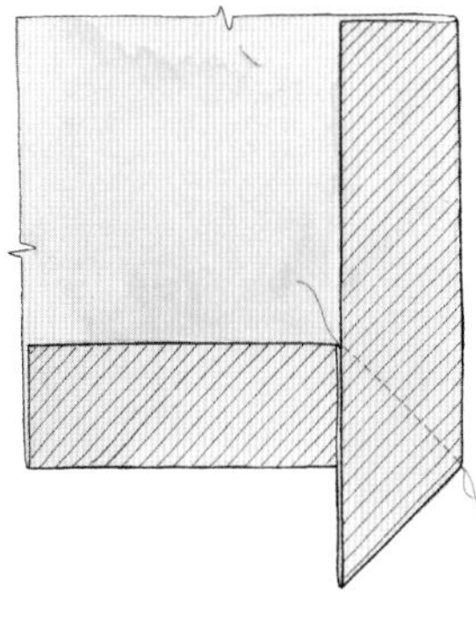

2

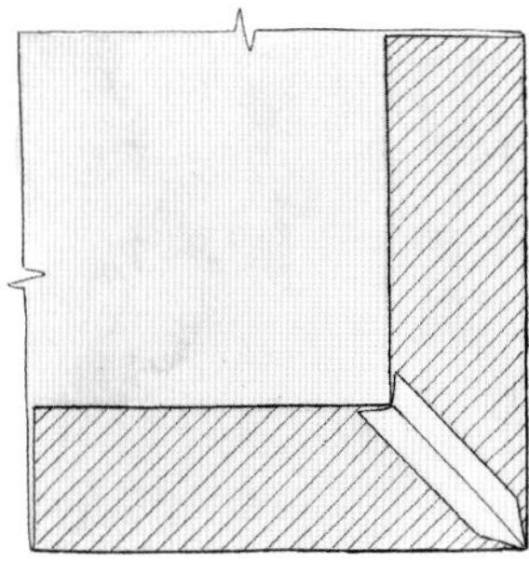

3

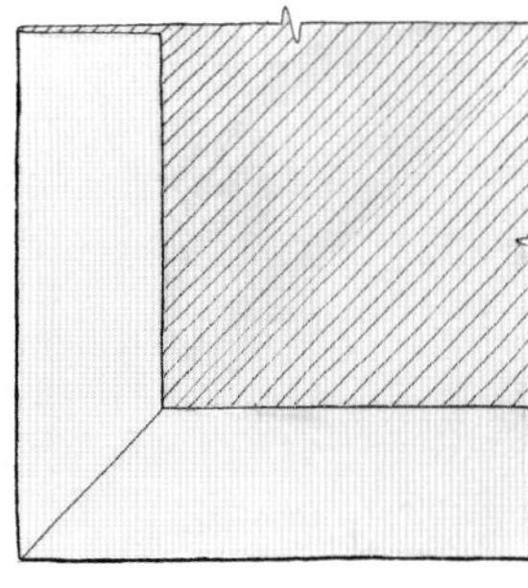

4

Mitering Applied Trim and Ribbon

Mark the placement lines for the trim with a water- or air-soluble pen (see page 16). Pin or glue the trim along the placement line until it meets the corner. Topstitch both edges of the trim, stopping at the corner.

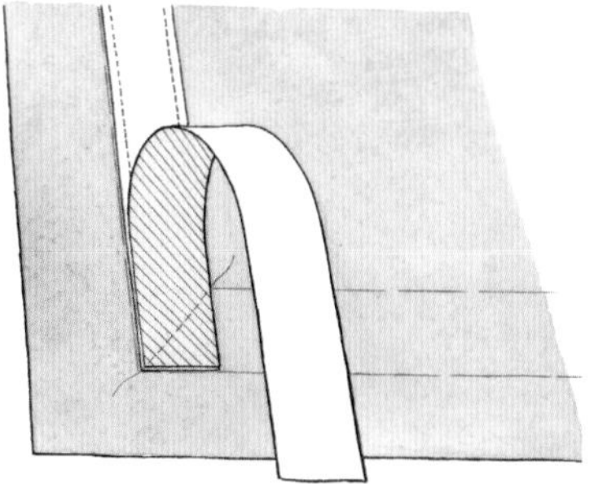

1

1. Fold the trim back on itself and finger-press. Fold the trim diagonally to form a right angle along the intersecting placement line. Refold the trim back on itself and stitch directly through the diagonal crease.

2. Fold the trim back down so it turns the corner smoothly and neatly. Press. Pin or glue the trim along the placement line. Topstitch along both edges.

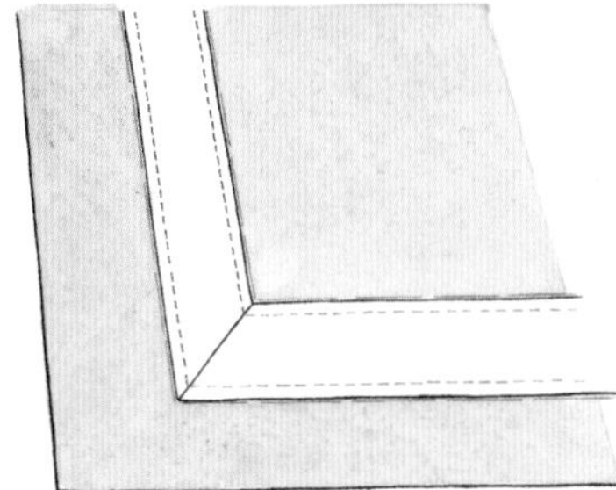

2

Do not pull trim taut. Stitch slowly, easing around corners so the trim lies flat.

forming gathers

Gathers are a series of tiny, soft folds of fabric that create shaping. Usually, you'll add gathers to garments at waistlines, yokes, sleeve caps, cuffs, and necklines.

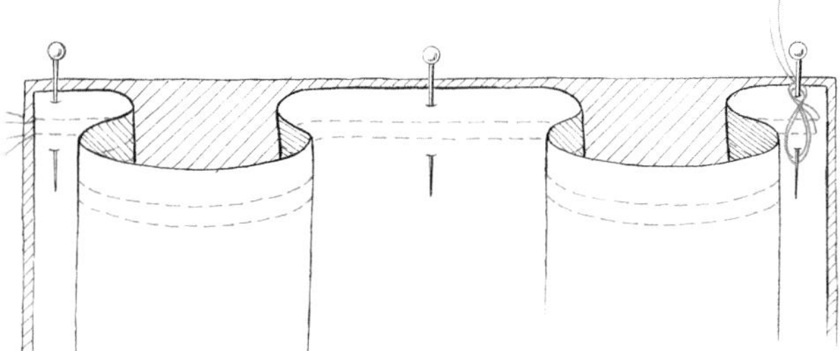

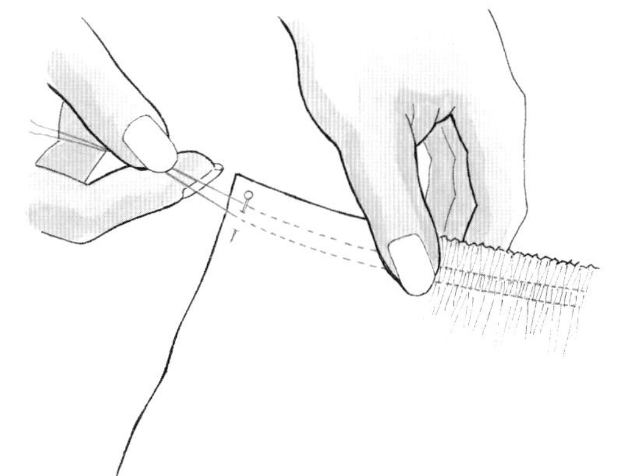

1 Set your machine to its longest straight stitch (the basting stitch). Loosen the upper thread tension slightly. Thread the bobbin with a contrasting color of thread for greater visibility.

2 On the right side of the fabric, stitch two parallel lines in the seam allowance: one just inside the stitching line and the other 1/4" (6 mm) away. Leave long thread tails at both ends. If the fabric is long, divide the area to be gathered in half and break the basting stitches at the halfway mark.

3 Pin the basted edge to its corresponding edge, right sides together. Match notches, seam lines, and markings. The piece with the basting stitches will be the longer piece. Secure the threads at one end by wrapping them around a straight pin to form a figure eight, as shown in the top drawing at left.

4 From the other end, pull the bobbin threads gently, sliding the fabric along the threads to distribute it evenly.

5 When the gathered piece "fits" the straight piece, pin the layers together at close intervals (about every 1/2" [1.3 cm]). As you work, adjust the gathers with a pin or with your fingernail so they are evenly distributed.

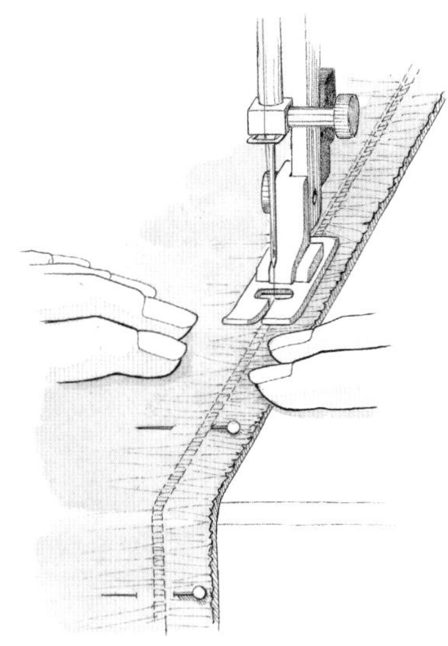

6 Change to a standard stitch length and normal upper-thread tension. With the gathered side up, machine-stitch a 5/8" (1.6 cm) seam. Remove pins as you sew—do not ever sew over pins! Hold the fabric taut with your fingertips on both sides of the needle to keep the gathers from shifting or pleating.

7 Open the garment and carefully press the seam allowances toward the flat, ungathered side with the tip of the iron. Do not press across the surface of the gathers or you will flatten them.

sewing ruffles

A ruffle is a strip of fabric that is gathered along one edge and attached to a flat piece of fabric—for example, on a skirt hem or the edge of a pillow. The visible edge is finished. The gathered raw edge is hidden in a seam or enclosed between two fabrics. Most ruffles are cut on the straight grain.

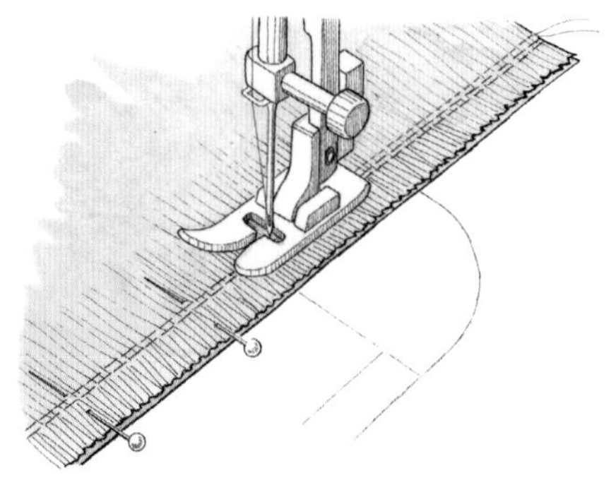

For a Hem Ruffle

1. Stitch the ruffle pieces together to form one long strip. Stitch a narrow hem on one long edge (see page 88). Press.

2. Sew two rows of basting stitches along the opposite long edge, just inside the seam line. Pull the threads to form gathers (see page 65).

3. Pin the ruffle with right sides together to the garment edge, aligning the raw edges and matching notches or dots. Adjust the gathers to distribute fullness evenly along the garment edge.

4. Stitch the ruffle in place. Remove the basting. Trim the seam allowances (see page 55). Zigzag-stitch or serge them together for a clean finish.

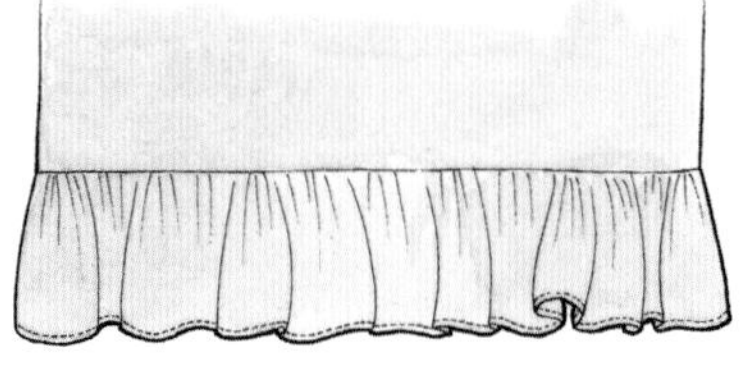

For an Enclosed Ruffle

1. Follow steps 1 to 3 above.

2. Stitch the ruffle to the first fabric, distributing the fullness evenly. Pin the second piece to the first, right sides together, with the ruffle in between. Stitch with the first piece up so you can use the existing stitching line as a guide.

3. Turn the pieces right side out. The ruffle will be along the outer edge.

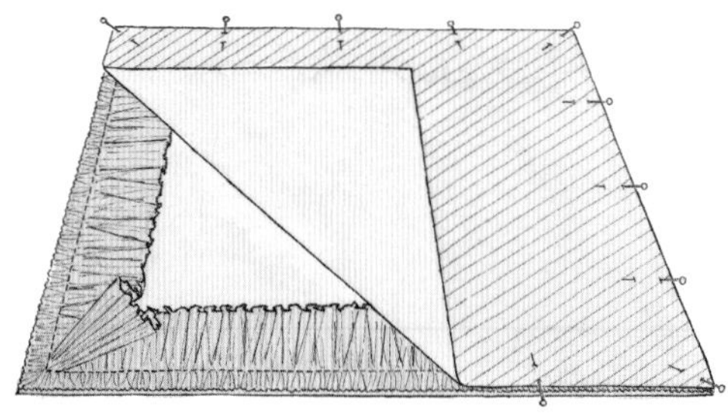

When applying a ruffle around corners, allow extra fullness at each corner so the ruffle lies flat.

easing

Some areas of a garment need only subtle shaping, which you can create by "easing" the seam. Unlike a gathered seam, an eased seam does not have any visible folds. Easing allows for a comfortable fit and ease of movement at shoulders, back yokes, elbows, sleeve caps, and inseams.

1. Set the machine stitch length to approximately 10 stitches per inch (2.5 cm). Fine fabrics requires a shorter stitch length. On the right side of the fabric, sew one row of stitching just inside the 5⁄8" (1.6 cm) stitching line for the required length of the eased area.

2. Pin the stitched edge to the corresponding piece of fabric so the edges and all markings align. Pull the bobbin thread gently to shorten the fabric and distribute the extra fabric fullness evenly. Pin every 1⁄4" to 1⁄2" (6 mm to 1.3 cm) along the easing line.

3. With a long machine stitch, baste the seam. Ease the fullness without stitching any folds into the seam. (Be patient! This takes a little practice.) Check the seam from the right side of the fabric. If you see any puckers or folds, remove the basting stitches and try again.

4. When the basted seam is perfect, shorten the stitch length and sew the pieces together, stitching over the basting stitches.

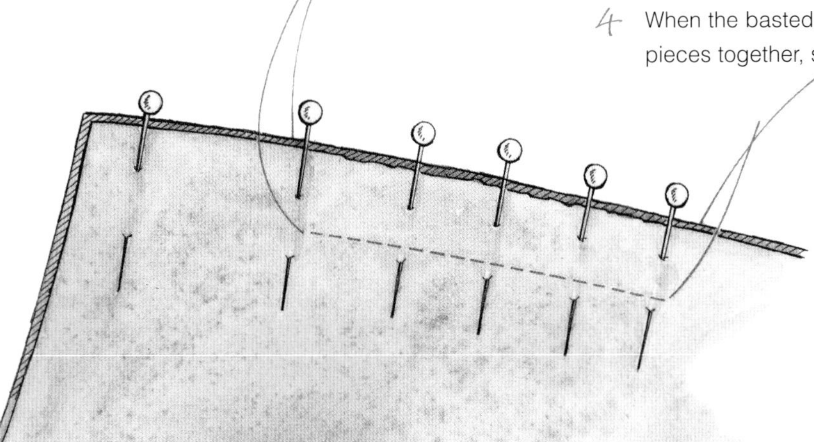

inserting a zipper

The zipper is one of the slickest inventions ever! There are several types of zippers (see pages 22 to 23), and each style is inserted into the garment in a slightly different way. The two most common ways zippers are inserted are with centered and lapped positioning. With a little patience and some tried-and-true tips, adding zippers can be a breeze.

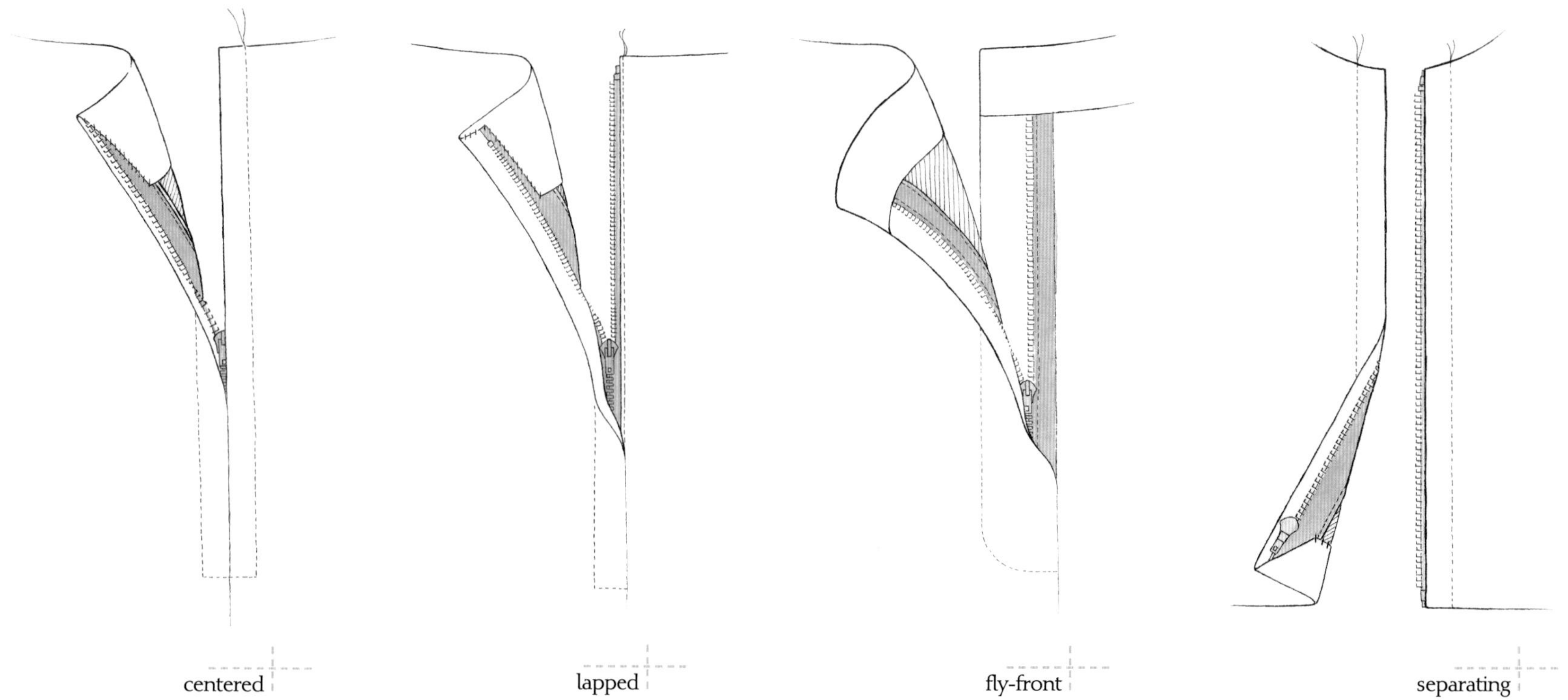

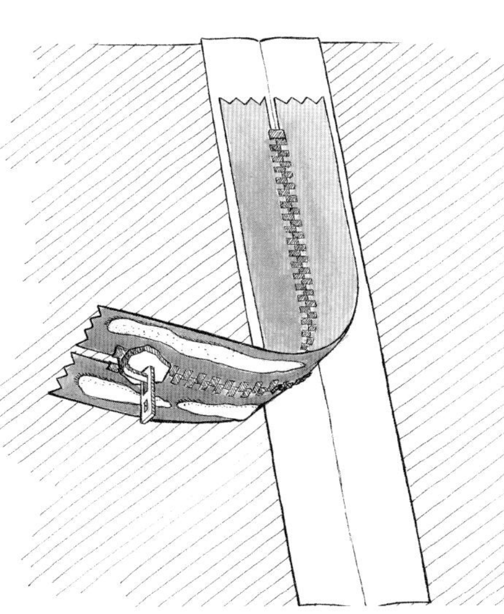

Preparing the Seam

It helps to have a little extra room in the seam allowances, so when you cut out the pattern, cut the zipper seam allowances to 3⁄4" (1.9 cm) instead of the usual 5⁄8" (1.6 cm). Clean-finish the raw edges before installing the zipper. You can extend narrow seam allowances by stitching seam binding to the raw edges. When working with stretch fabric, stabilize the zipper area by fusing a narrow strip of interfacing to the wrong side of each seam allowance.

Before Inserting the Zipper

Remove the zipper from the package and press out the folds with a cool iron. Attach a zipper foot to your machine and adjust the needle position or foot position so the needle will be between the foot and the zipper teeth. Basting tape or fabric glue will temporarily hold the zipper in place on the seam to make it easier to stitch.

When sewing a zipper, flip up the pull tab to stitch past it more easily.

inserting a lapped zipper

Lapped zipper construction conceals the zipper and is most often used at side seams or at the center backs of dresses, skirts, and pants. (If the zipper is in a curved side seam, use a coil zipper, which is more flexible, and press it on a tailor's ham.)

1. Follow step 1 for the centered zipper construction (page 72). Attach the zipper foot and adjust so it is to the right of the needle. Open the zipper and place it facedown on the right-hand side of the seam allowance (with the open end facing you). Position the zipper coil directly over the seam line and the top stop 1" (2.5 cm) below the cut edge. Flip up the tab. Pin, glue, or hand-baste the zipper tape to the seam allowance only.

2. Machine-baste from the bottom to the top of the zipper, as close to the edge of the coil as possible.

3. Close the zipper, turn the zipper faceup, and flip up the pull tab. Smooth the fabric away from the zipper, forming a narrow fold between the coil and the seam. Adjust the zipper foot to the left of the needle and, starting at the bottom of the zipper, stitch through the folded seam allowance and the zipper tape, as close to the edge of the fold as possible.

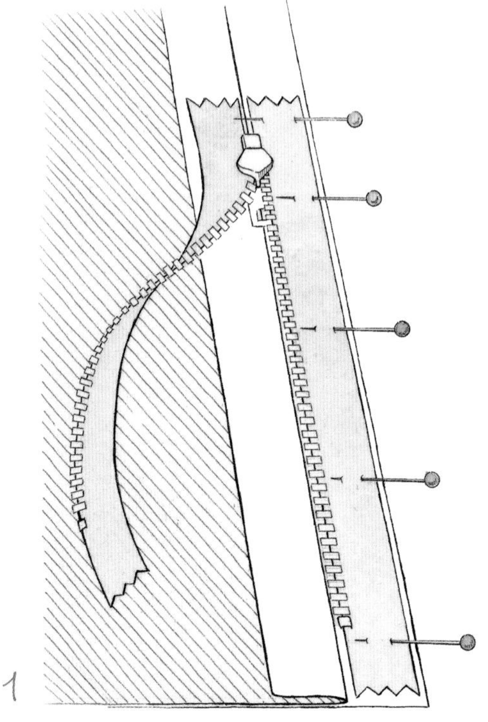

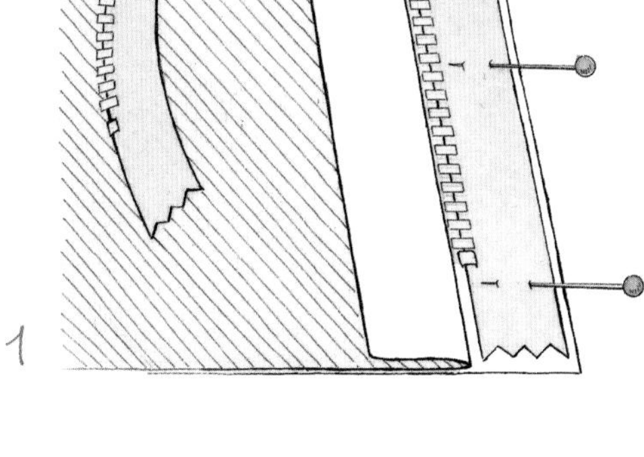

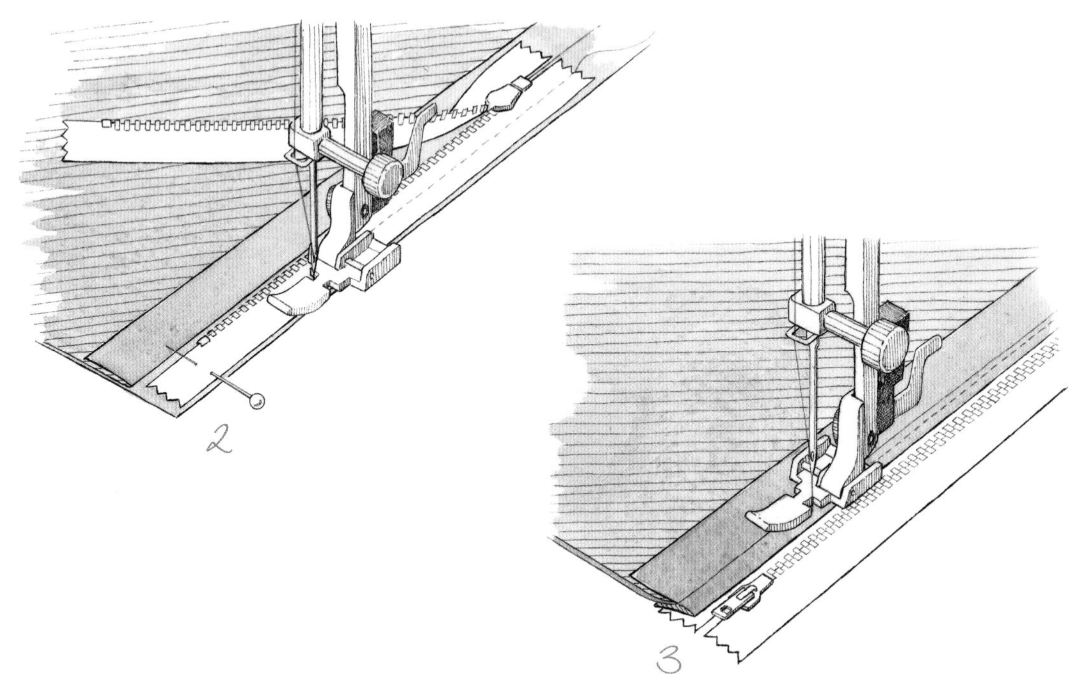

4 Turn the garment to the right side and spread the fabric as flat as possible. Mark the bottom of the zipper with a pin. Place 1/2" (1.3 cm) wide clear tape along the right side of the seam to act as a topstitching guide. Starting at the seam line at the bottom of the zipper, topstitch across the bottom and up the outside edge of the tape.

5 Remove the tape. Pull the thread tails to the wrong side and knot them. Remove the basting stitches and press. Press on a tailor's ham if the seam is curved.

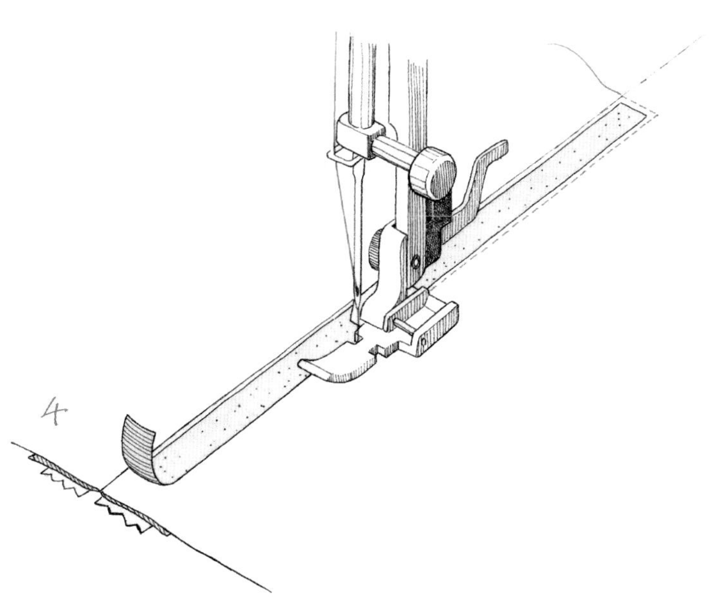

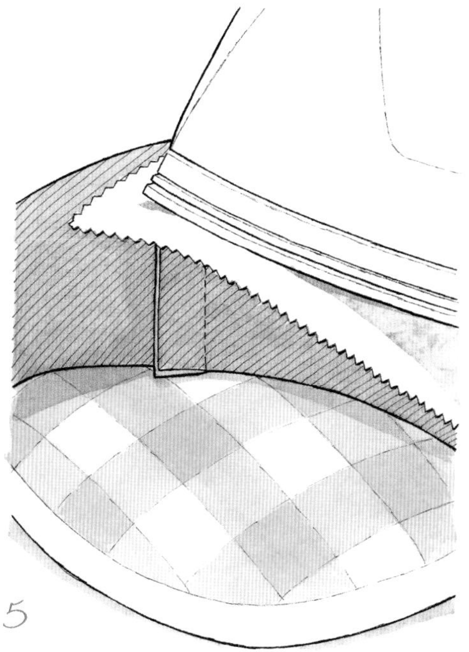

inserting a centered zipper

Centered zippers are typically sewn in home décor items and in the center front or center back of a garment.

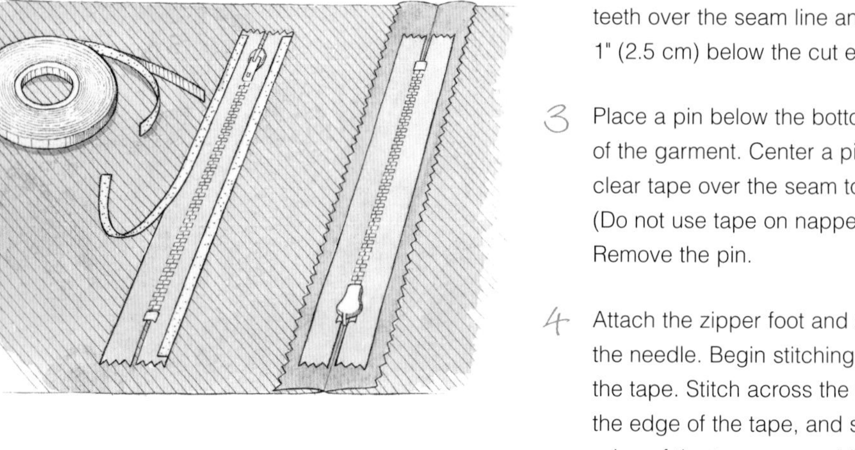

2

1 Machine-baste the zipper opening closed. Clip the basting stitches every 2" (5.1 cm) so they can be easily removed later. Press the seam open. Finish the seam allowance edges with pinking or zigzag stitches (see page 58).

2 Use a glue stick or basting tape to position the zipper facedown on the wrong side of the garment. Center the teeth over the seam line and position the top stop 1" (2.5 cm) below the cut edge. Flip up the pull tab.

3 Place a pin below the bottom stop on the right side of the garment. Center a piece of 1/2" (1.3 cm) wide clear tape over the seam to act as a stitching guide. (Do not use tape on napped or delicate fabrics.) Remove the pin.

4 Attach the zipper foot and adjust so it is to the right of the needle. Begin stitching at the seam at the bottom of the tape. Stitch across the bottom of the zipper, pivot at the edge of the tape, and stitch up the side, using the edge of the tape as a guide.

5 Adjust the zipper foot to the left of the needle. Again begin stitching at the seam at the bottom of the tape. Stitch up the opposite side of the zipper.

6 Pull the thread tails to the wrong side and knot them at the bottom of the zipper. Remove the basting stitches and press with a press cloth.

4

5

buttonhole tips

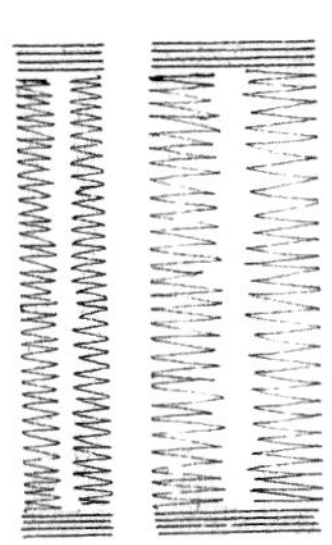

Computerized machines make automatic, one-step buttonholes in several styles—but you can make quality buttonholes on any type of machine with a simple zigzag stitch. Use a wide zigzag stitch for heavier fabrics and a narrow one for lightweight fabrics. To prevent the buttonhole from gaping or puckering, stabilize it with similar color interfacing. If the fabric is sheer or lightweight, use a tear-away stabilizer so you can remove it later. For button styles, see page 24.

What Makes a Good Buttonhole?

- The thread and garment color match.
- The button weight is compatible with the weight of the fabric, thread, and interfacing/stabilizer.
- Each buttonhole lies smooth and flat without puckering.
- Interfacing or stabilizer is not visible, but simply supports the stitches.
- All the buttonholes are evenly spaced.
- All the buttonholes are the same length and width.
- The buttonholes are 1/8" (3 mm) longer than the button.

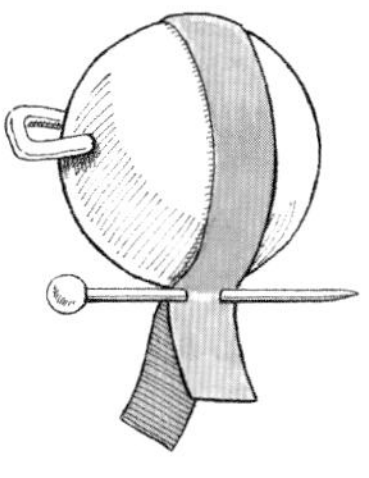

To Determine Buttonhole Length

flat button: Measure the diameter and thickness of the button. Add 1/8" (3 mm) to these numbers.

shank button: Pin a thin strip of paper around the button. Slide the button out and measure between the pin marks. Add 1/8" (3 mm) to this number.

For extra stability, apply a patch of fusible web to the wrong side of the buttonhole area.

making buttonholes

Horizontal buttonholes—perpendicular to the garment edge—are best for jackets and coats. Vertical buttonholes—parallel to the edge—are used on plackets, shirt bands, and with small buttons.

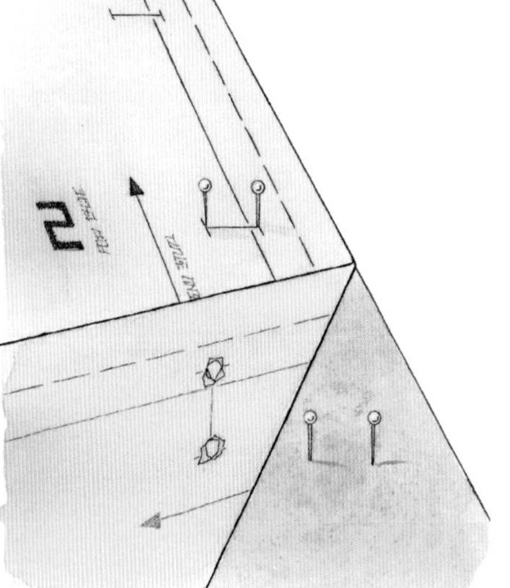

How to Make a Buttonhole

1 Place the pattern tissue over the garment, aligning the pattern seam line with the garment opening. Insert pins to mark the position of the buttonholes on the right side of the garment.

2 Carefully remove the pattern. Mark the buttonhole positions with pins, hand-basting, or a fabric-marking pen (see page 16).

3 To make a four-step buttonhole, start with a full bobbin, new needle, and buttonhole foot. Lower the foot over the center marking. Stitch three or four stitches across the end to form the first bar tack (the stitching at one end of the buttonhole).

4 Stitch down one side to the other marked end. Stitch three or four wider stitches to form the bar tack on the other end of the buttonhole.

5 Stitch up the opposite side, stopping at the bar tack. Make one or two small stitches in place to secure the threads.

6 Insert pins across the buttonhole, just inside each bar tack so you won't cut through them when you open the buttonhole. With small, sharp scissors or a seam ripper, carefully cut the fabric between the lines of stitching.

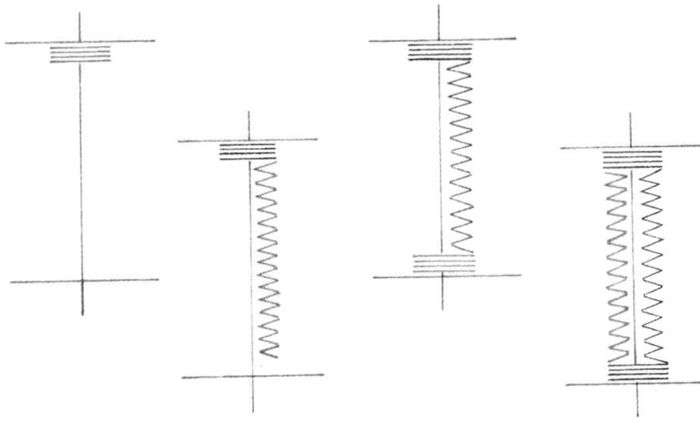

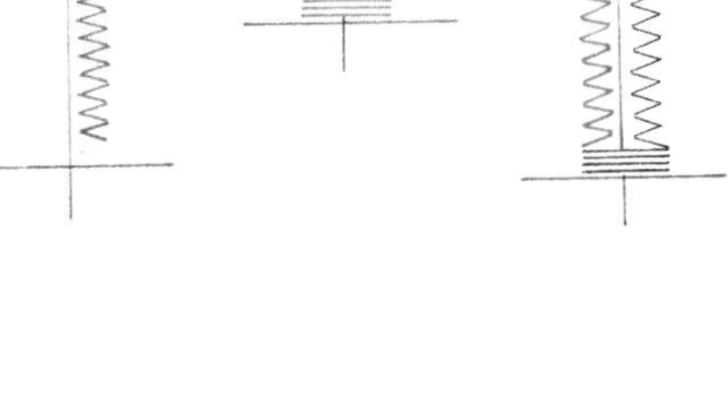

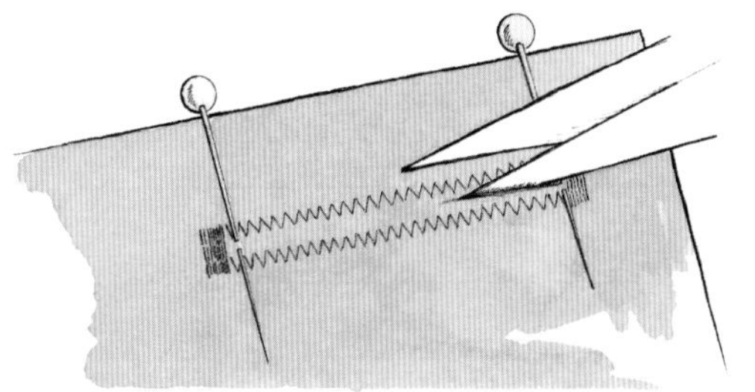

sewing on buttons

Make sure you position buttons in the right locations so the garment closes correctly and lies flat. Mark their positions carefully on the right side of the garment. Lap the buttonholes over the button area, measuring to the amount indicated by the pattern. Push a pin through the buttonhole ⅛" (3 mm) from the end to mark the button location. Hand-stitch with a doubled length of all-purpose thread for light- and medium-weight fabrics and a doubled length of heavy-duty thread for heavier fabrics.

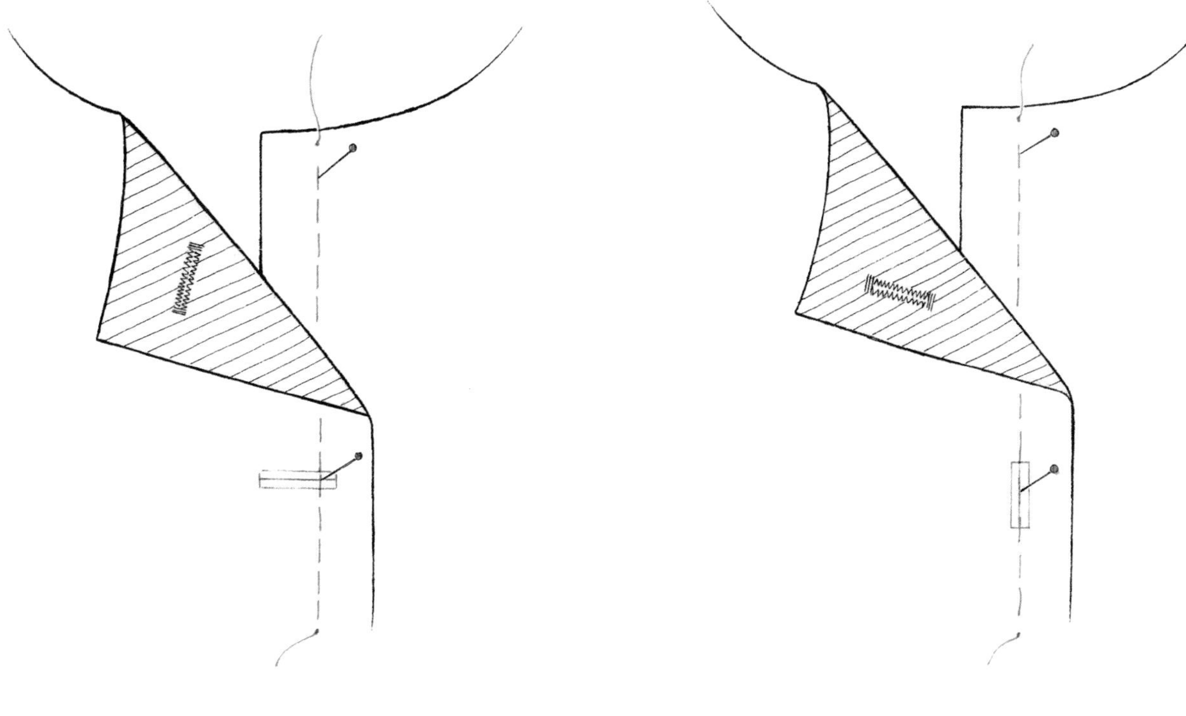

Flat Button

(for lightweight fabrics and decorative styles)

1. Thread the needle and knot the ends.
2. Bring the needle through one hole and back down through the opposite hole and the fabric several times. If there are four holes, stitch through the other two holes the same way.
3. Knot the thread on the wrong side of the fabric.

Flat Button with Thread Shank

(for medium- to heavy-weight fabrics)

1. Thread the needle and knot the ends. Bring the needle up at the mark from the wrong side and insert it through one button hole. Place a toothpick on top of the button. Bring the needle down through the opposite hole. Take about six stitches. If there are four holes, do the same for the other two holes.
2. Remove the toothpick and lift the button away from the fabric. Bring the needle out between the button and the fabric surface. Wind the thread around the stitches to create a thread shank. Take two or three tiny stitches on the wrong side of the fabric to secure and knot the ends.

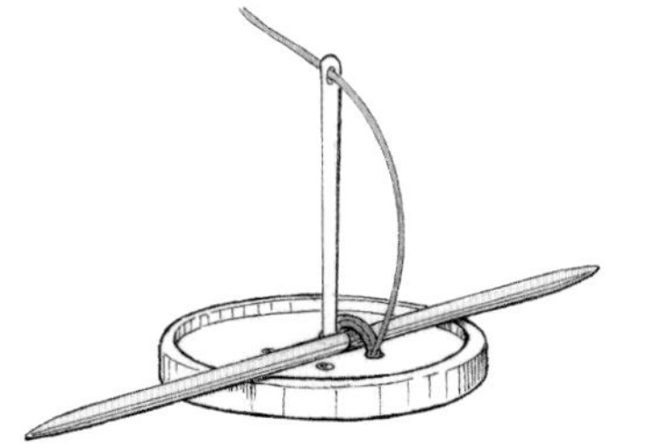

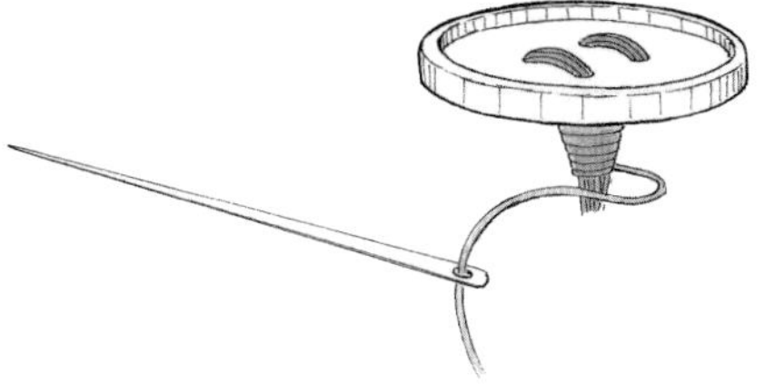

Shank Button

(for medium- to heavy-weight fabrics)

1. Thread the needle and knot the ends.
2. Position the button with the shank perpendicular to the garment. Attach the button by sewing several stitches through the shank. Take two or three tiny stitches on the wrong side of the fabric and knot the ends.

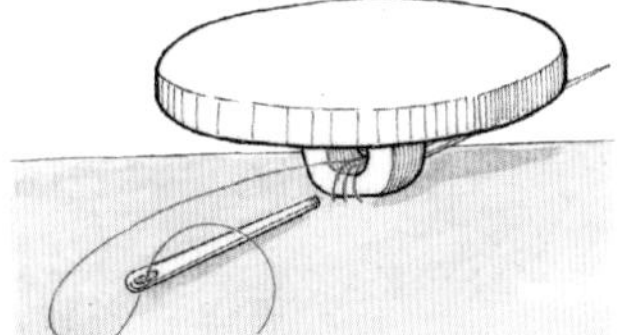

attaching fasteners

There are many other fasteners—beyond the basic button—for keeping garments closed. Make sure the weight and size of the fastener is compatible with the weight of your fabric.

toggles and frogs: Slipstitch these fasteners faceup, with the loop extending over the garment edge. Take small invisible slipstitches (see page 60) around the trim.

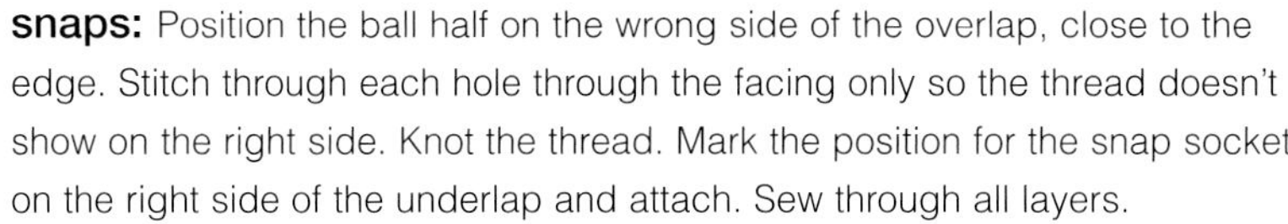

snaps: Position the ball half on the wrong side of the overlap, close to the edge. Stitch through each hole through the facing only so the thread doesn't show on the right side. Knot the thread. Mark the position for the snap socket on the right side of the underlap and attach. Sew through all layers.

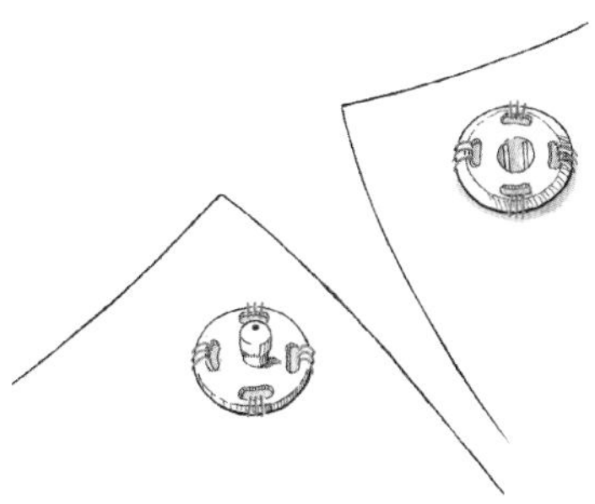

hook-and-loop tape: This style fastener is applied to overlapping edges. Position the hook tape on the right side of the underlap. Edgestitch around the perimeter. Align the loop tape on the wrong side of the overlap. Edgestitch around the perimeter.

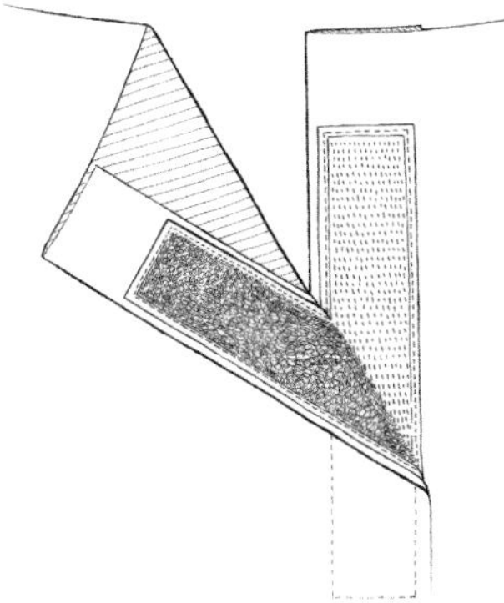

hooks and eyes: Sew the hook to the wrong side of the overlap, without stitching through to the right side. Stitch several times over each hole. Close the garment. Mark the position of the end of the hook on the right side of the underlap. Sew the eye at the mark.

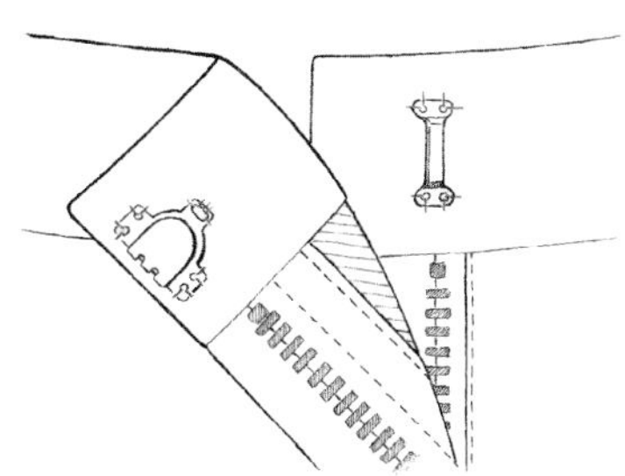

sewing elastic to fabric

You can sew lengths of elastic directly to the wrong side of the fabric to shape a garment at wrists, ankles, and waistlines. Choose woven or knitted elastic that is soft enough to wear close to your skin. Cut it slightly shorter than you need because it stretches during sewing. Sew with a stretch stitch or a zigzag stitch, which will stretch along with the elastic.

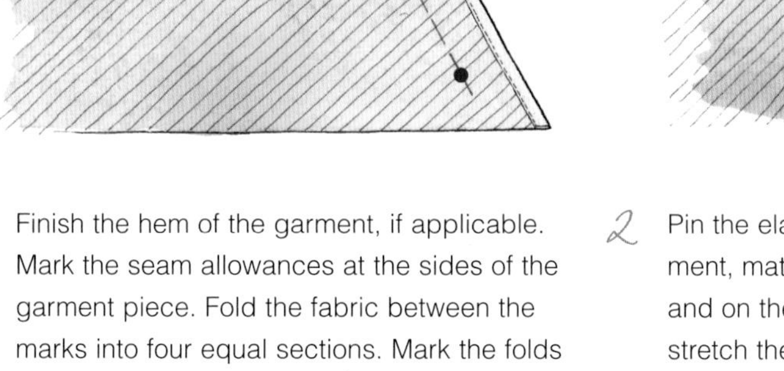

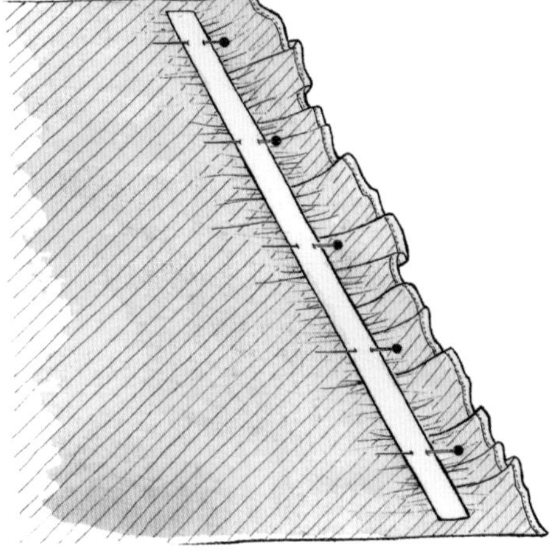

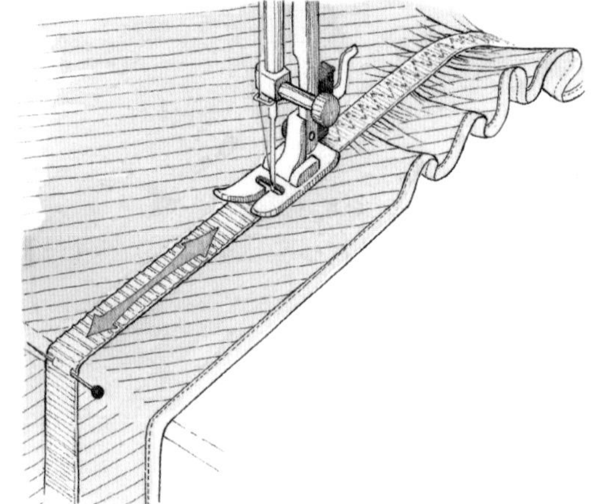

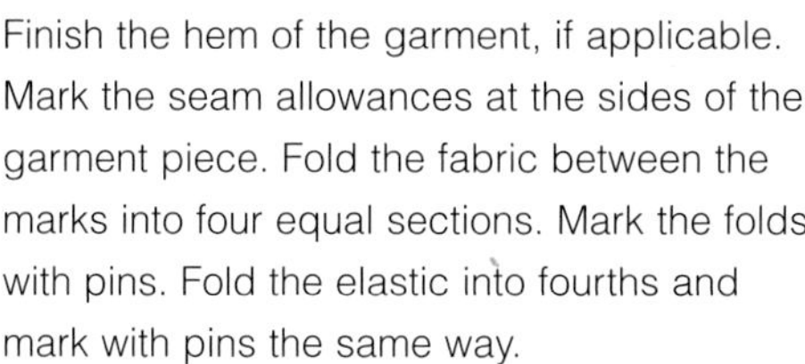

1 Finish the hem of the garment, if applicable. Mark the seam allowances at the sides of the garment piece. Fold the fabric between the marks into four equal sections. Mark the folds with pins. Fold the elastic into fourths and mark with pins the same way.

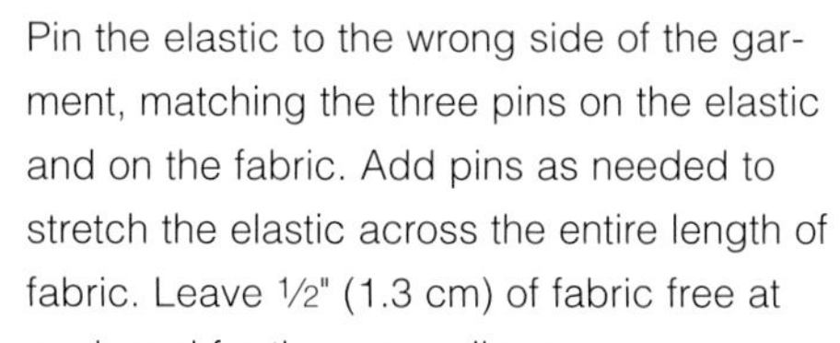

2 Pin the elastic to the wrong side of the garment, matching the three pins on the elastic and on the fabric. Add pins as needed to stretch the elastic across the entire length of fabric. Leave ½" (1.3 cm) of fabric free at each end for the seam allowance.

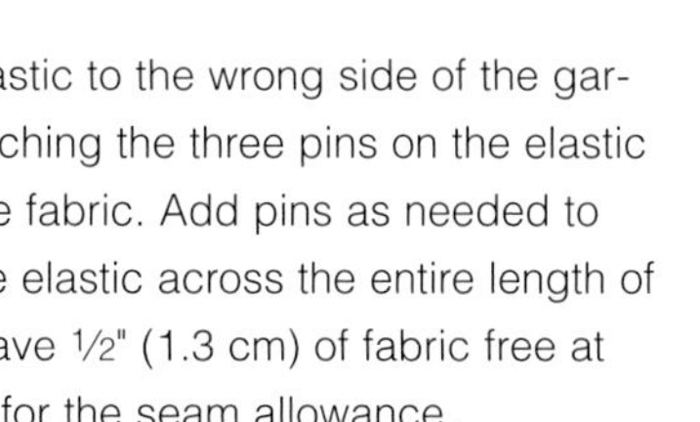

3 Stitch the elastic to the fabric, stretching the elastic between the pins. Hold the fabric taut with one hand behind the presser foot and the other in front. Let the feed dogs move the fabric as you sew.

inserting elastic in a casing

Elastic is sometimes inserted in a fabric tunnel called a casing. You can create a casing by folding and stitching the fabric at a garment edge. Or you can apply a band of tricot (sheer ribbon) or bias tape (see page 28) close to the garment edge—at the waistline of a dress, for example.

To determine how much elastic you need, wrap the elastic strip around your body and add 1" (2.5 cm) for finishing the ends. Braided and non-roll elastic won't twist inside the casing.

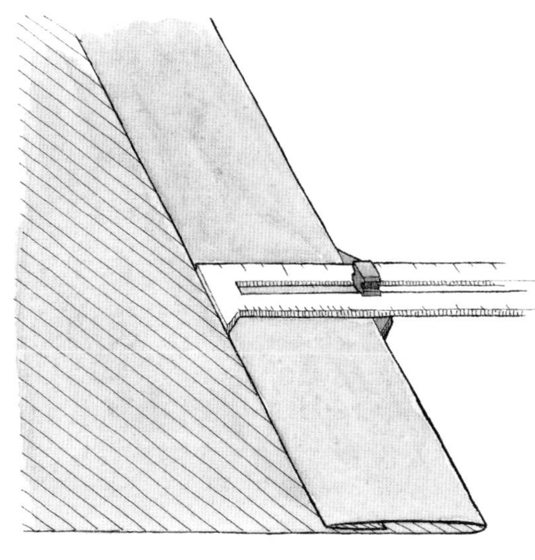

1

Edge Casing

1. Press the garment edge ½" (1.3 cm) to the wrong side. Fold the fabric again the desired amount to form the casing. Make the casing ¼" (6 mm) wider than the elastic for easy insertion.

2. Edgestitch close to the top fold. Edgestitch close to the bottom fold, leaving a 2" (5.1 cm) opening near one side seam.

3. Secure a safety pin to one end of the elastic and insert it into the casing opening. Push and pull the safety pin through the casing until it reaches the opening. Make sure that the opposite end of the elastic doesn't get pulled into the casing.

4. Feel along the casing to make sure the elastic is not twisted. Overlap the ends of the elastic and hand-stitch them together or machine-stitch with a zigzag stitch.

5. Stretch the elastic to pull the ends into the casing. Edgestitch the opening closed, being careful not to catch the elastic in the stitches.

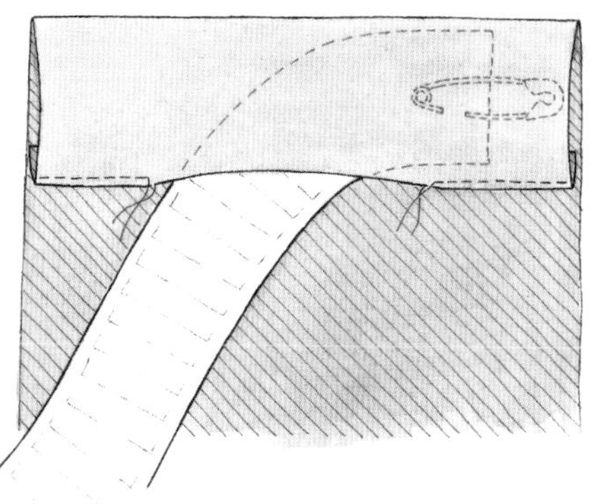

3

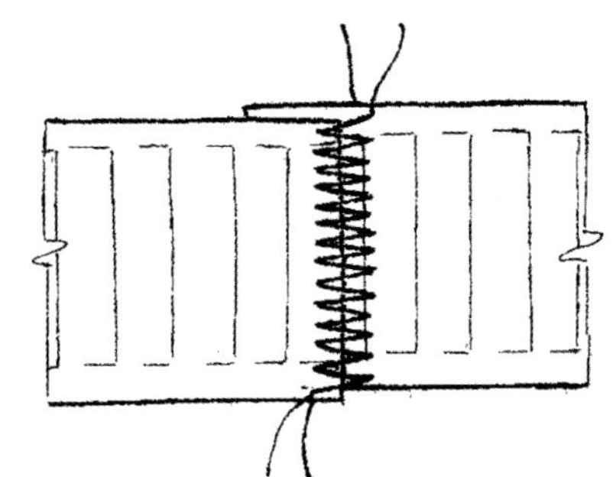

Applied Casing

1 Pin bias tape or a strip of tricot that is 1/4" (6 mm) wider than the elastic over the marked casing line. Press under the ends 1/4" (6 mm) and abut the folds. Stitch close to both long edges.

2 Insert the elastic and stitch the ends together as for the edge casing (page 79, steps 3 and 4). Ease the elastic back into the casing. Slipstitch the casing ends closed.

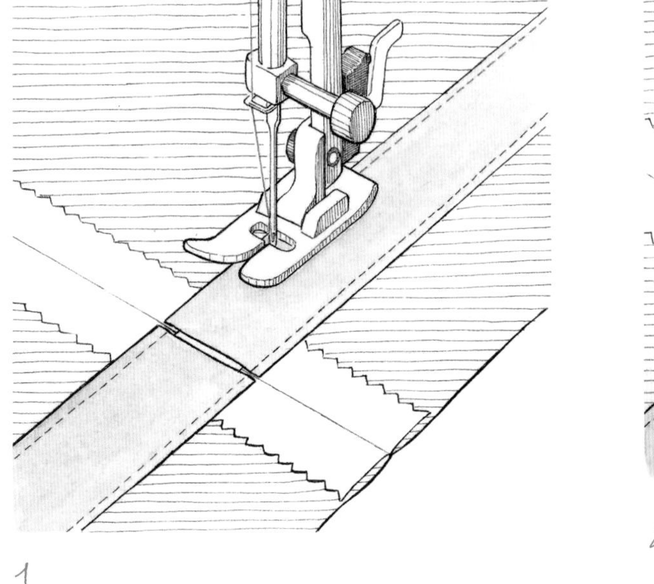

1

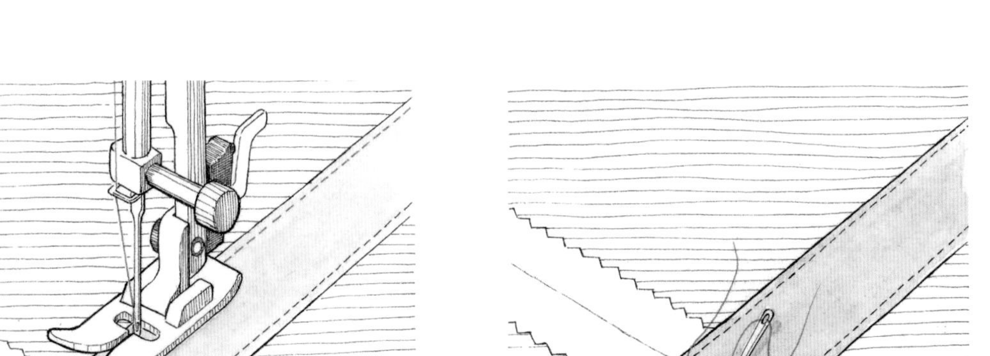

2

making bias binding

Bias binding encloses fabric edges for a neat, often decorative, finish. Because of the bias grain direction, the binding wraps around curves without puckering. You can make either a single-fold or double-fold binding.

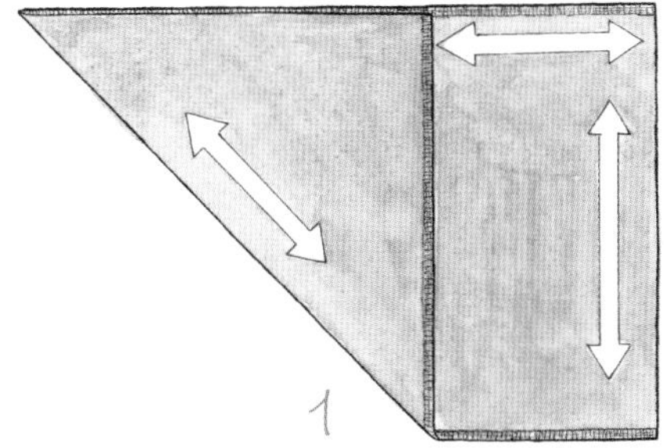

1

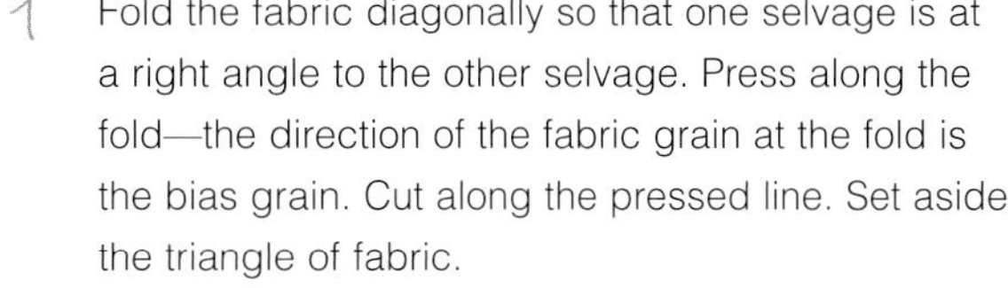

1 Fold the fabric diagonally so that one selvage is at a right angle to the other selvage. Press along the fold—the direction of the fabric grain at the fold is the bias grain. Cut along the pressed line. Set aside the triangle of fabric.

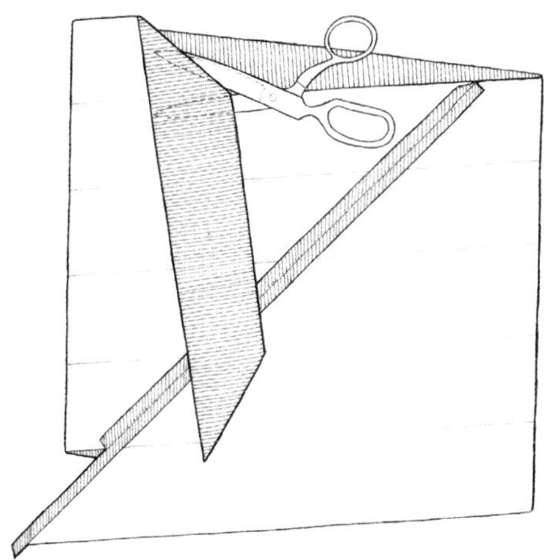

3

2 Multiply the desired finished width of the binding by four to determine how wide to cut the strips. For example, for 1⁄4" (6 mm) finished binding, you'll need strips 1" (2.5 cm) wide. Beginning at the diagonal cut edge of the fabric, measure and mark parallel lines that are the desired cutting width. After you have drawn the last strip, discard the triangular remnant—or save it as scrap.

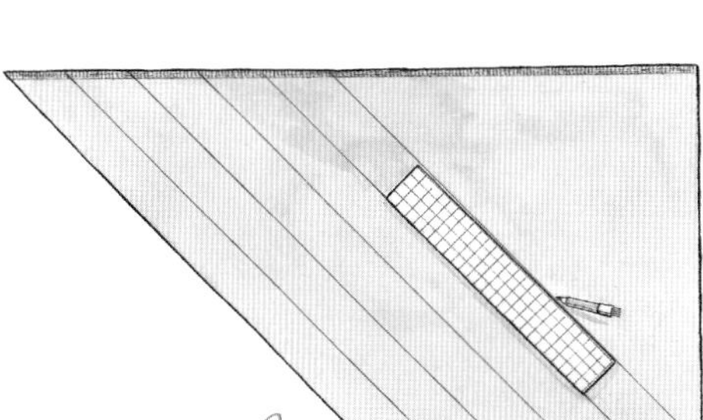

2

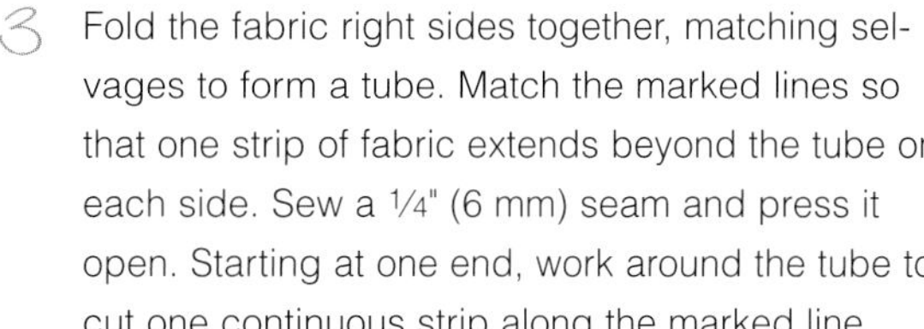

3 Fold the fabric right sides together, matching selvages to form a tube. Match the marked lines so that one strip of fabric extends beyond the tube on each side. Sew a 1⁄4" (6 mm) seam and press it open. Starting at one end, work around the tube to cut one continuous strip along the marked line.

4 Press both long edges to the center of the tape, taking care not to distort the width of the strip. Press the strip in half again to create the double fold.

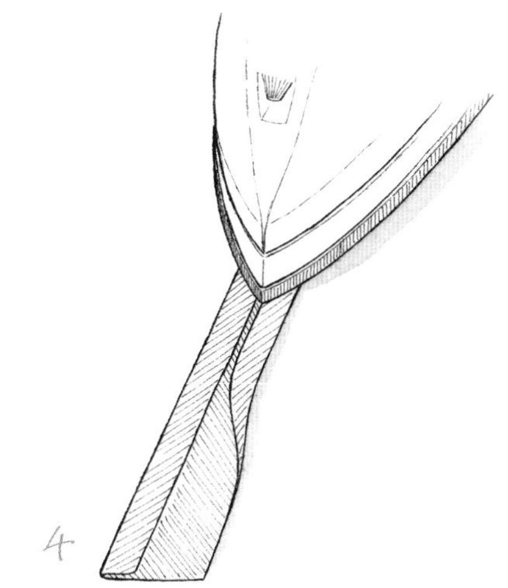

4

making piping

Piping is a bias fabric wrapped around a narrow polyester or cotton cord. You sew piping into a seam for a well-defined edge finish. You can purchase piping in an assortment of colors. For a perfect match, it's easy make your own.

1. Cut bias strips as you would when making bias binding (page 81, steps 1 to 3). The width of the strip should be two times the seam allowance plus the circumference of the cord. Allow extra length so you can overlap the ends and ease the piping around corners as you sew.

2. Attach a zipper foot or piping foot to your machine. Wrap the bias strip, right side out, around the cord, keeping the raw edges even. Stitch right next to the cord, gently stretching the fabric as you sew.

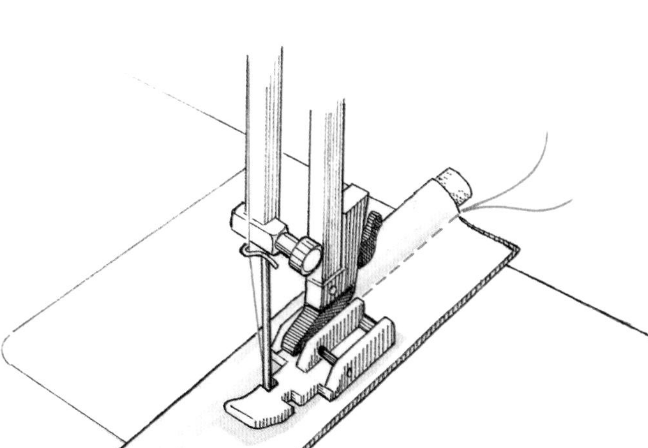

attaching trims

Decorative trims give your garments style and provide a way to add your own personal touch. Some trims—like bias tape—are also helpful in construction. There are several application methods, depending on the style of the trim and the way it is used.

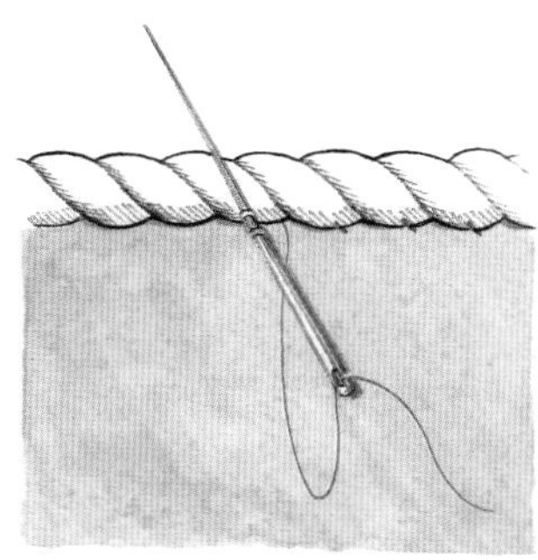

hand-stitched trim: Raised trim must be attached by hand. Slipstitch (see page 60) the trim to the fabric with thread that is the same color as the fabric.

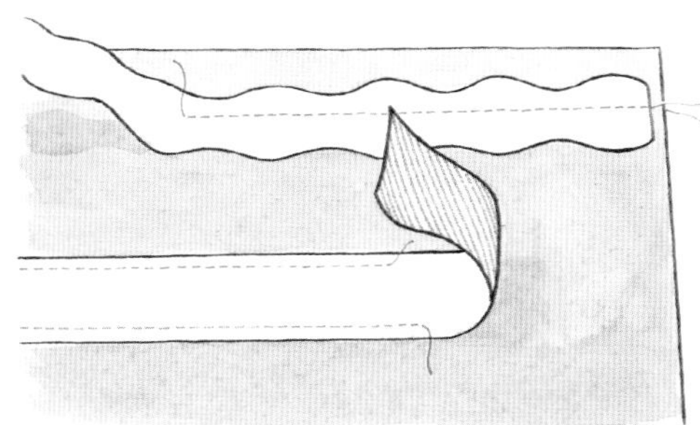

machine-stitched band trim: Secure the trim in place with basting tape or fabric adhesive. If the trim is less than 1/4" (6 mm) wide, machine-stitch down the center. If it is wider than 1/4" (6 mm), machine-stitch both long edges in the same direction.

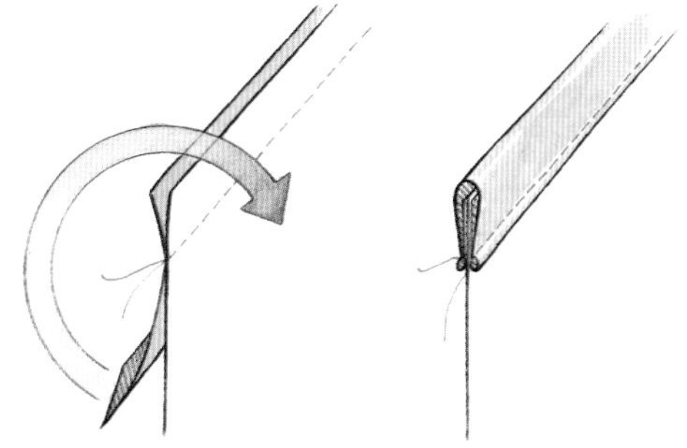

bias tape: Open the tape and, with right sides together, pin it to the fabric, matching cut edges. Stitch along the fold line closest to the raw edge.

Fold the binding up and over to encase the raw edge. On the right side of the fabric, edgestitch (see page 52) the binding in place. (This stitching will catch the underneath layer, which is slightly wider than the top layer.)

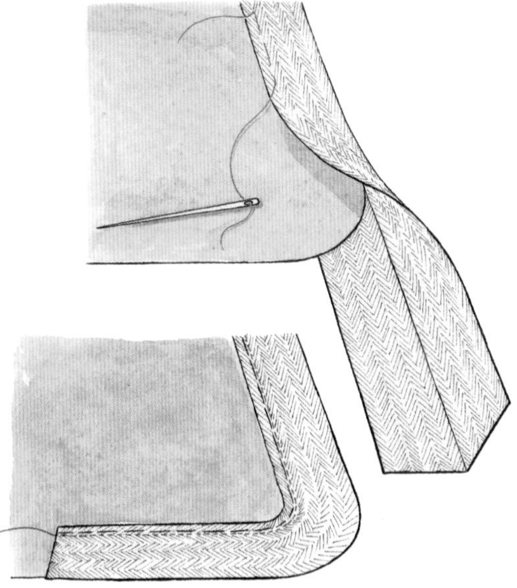

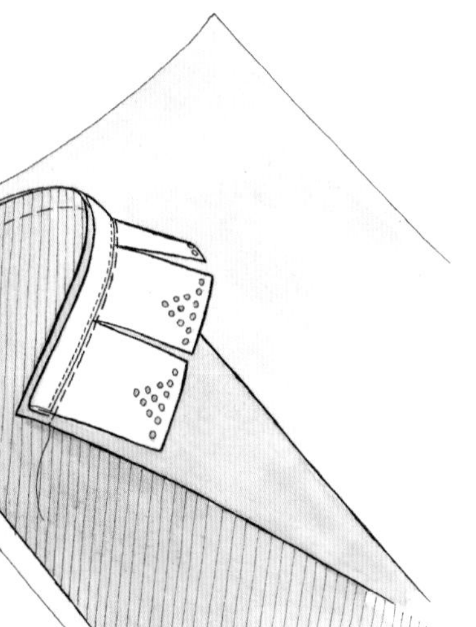

fold-over braid: With the narrower edge on the right side of the fabric, encase the raw edge with the braid. Hand-baste (see page 61) through all layers. Topstitch close to the inside edge.

edging in a seam: Working on the right side of the fabric, align the unfinished edge of the trim with the raw edge of the fabric, with seam lines matching. Baste. Pin the two fabric layers together with the trim in between. Stitch. Use a zipper foot if the trim doesn't lie flat.

edging along a finished edge: Position the wrong side of the folded or hemmed fabric edge on top of the edging and topstitch. Or sew the trim on the right side of the fabric and cover the seam with ribbon.

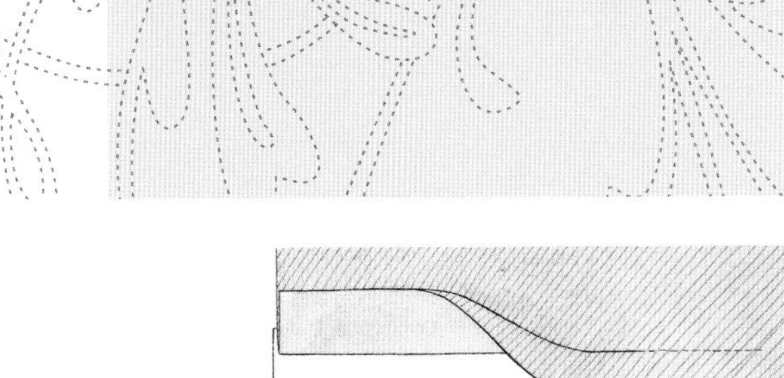

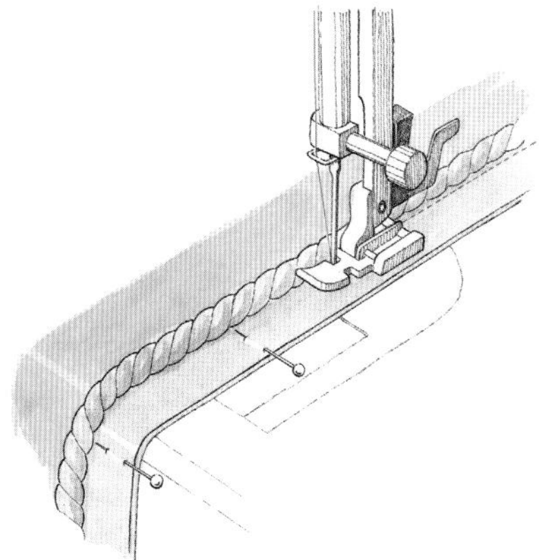

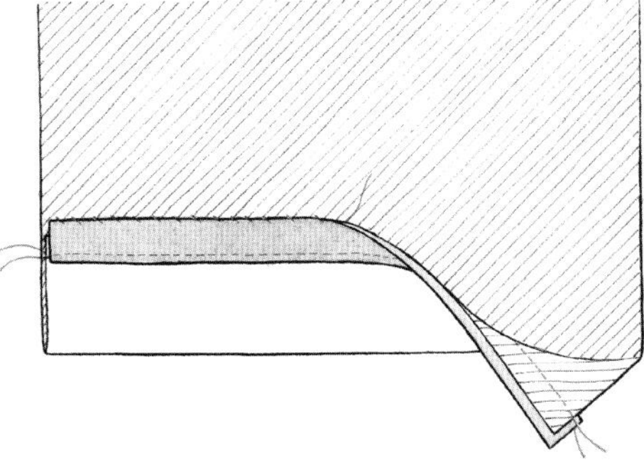

insertion trim: Pin or glue the trim to the right side of the fabric and topstitch it along both straight edges (in the same direction). From the wrong side, cut the fabric down the center, between the two rows of stitching, to create seam allowances. Press the seam allowances away from each other, exposing the trim. Edgestitch though all layers close to the folds. Trim the seam allowances close to the edgestitching.

seam binding/seam tape: To hem loosely woven fabrics, stitch the edge of the tape or binding 1⁄4" (6 mm) from the raw edge of the fabric. To clean-finish loosely woven seam allowances, press the tape or binding in half and wrap it over the raw edge. Edgestitch in place.

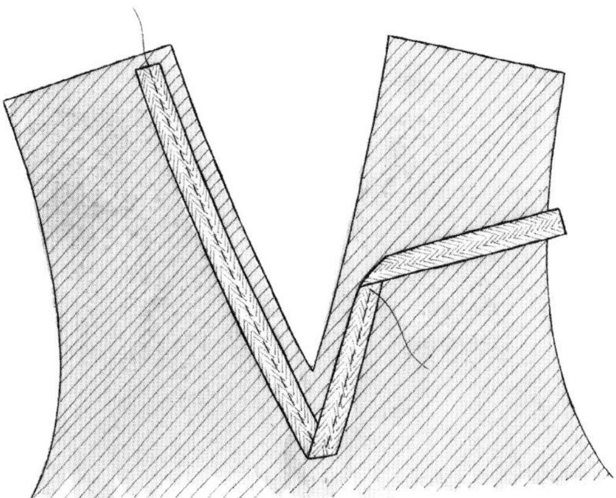

piping: Apply piping just as you would edging in a seam. Attach the zipper foot so you can stitch as close to the trim as possible. (To make your own piping, see page 82.)

twill tape: To reinforce a seam, center twill tape over the seam line, inside the garment, and stitch it in place. To extend seam allowances, machine-stitch one edge of the tape to the raw edge of the fabric.

marking & preparing hems

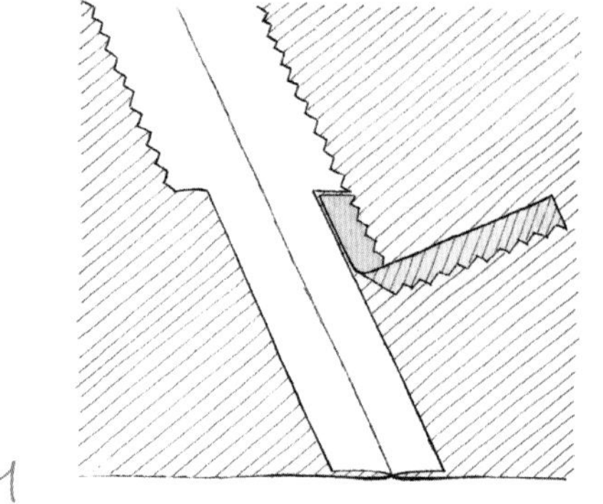

1

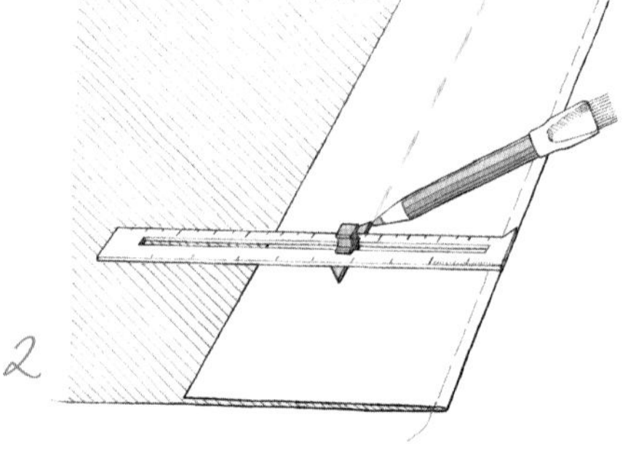

2

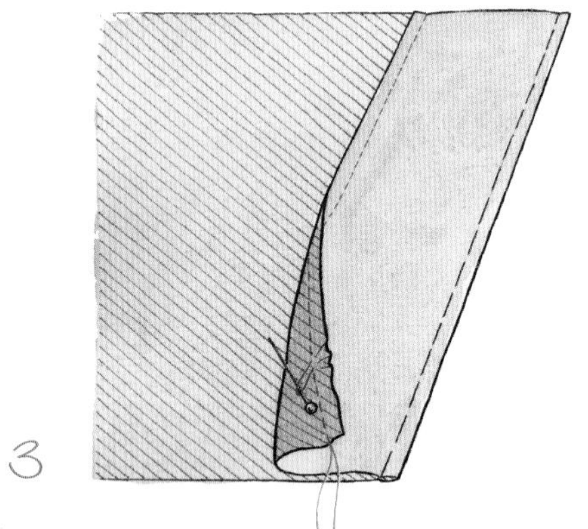

3

You can stitch hems by machine or by hand. Some hems should be invisible on the right side of the garment, but others are meant to be seen. For a straight garment, the hem allowance can be up to 3" (7.6 cm) wide. For a flared garment, the hem is usually from 1½" to 2" (3.8 to 5.1 cm) wide. Sheer fabrics and lightweight knits almost always have narrow hems stitched by machine.

Marking a Hem

Put on the garment, with all the appropriate undergarments and accessories. Enlist the help of a friend to chalk or pin-mark the hem an even distance from the floor. Stand in one place while your helper moves around you, measuring with a yardstick (meterstick) and marking.

Pin up the entire hem to make sure you like the length. Make adjustments as needed.

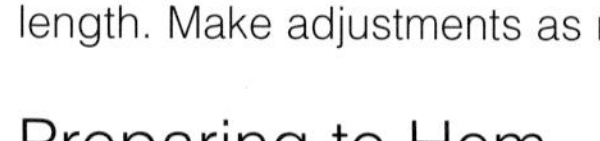

Preparing to Hem

1. Trim seam allowances below the marked hemline to reduce bulk.
2. Fold up the hem along the marks and hand-baste it to the fabric, close to the fold. Measure and mark the desired hem depth from the fold. Add ¼" (6 mm) if you are clean-finishing the edge. Trim away the excess fabric.
3. If the hem is curved, stitch only ¼" (6 mm) from the raw edge with a long machine stitch. Pull up the bobbin thread every few inches to ease the fullness.

To Clean-Finish the Edge

If your fabric tends to ravel, you may want to clean-finish the edge before you hem.

- Turn under ¼" (6 mm) to the wrong side and press the fold. Machine-stitch.
- Machine-straight-stitch ¼" (6 mm) from the edge. Trim the edge with pinking shears.
- Zigzag or overcast the raw edge.
- Edgestitch a seam binding or hem tape to the right side of the garment edge, overlapping the short ends.

If your garment is cut on the bias, hang it on a hanger for 24 hours before marking the hem. The fabric will relax to its true length.

hemming methods

After you have marked and prepared the garment hem, you're ready to stitch the hem in place. You can hem in several ways, either by hand or machine. You can also fuse the hem on some fabrics. For hand and machine stitches, see pages 52, 53, and 60.

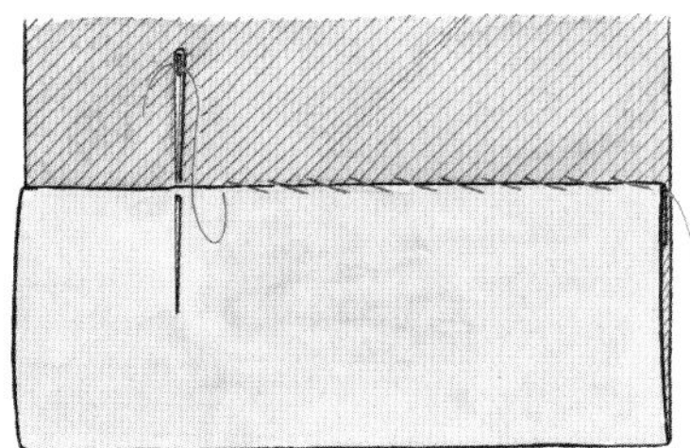

Hemming by Hand

hand blindstitch: Fold back the top edge of the hem. Take a tiny stitch in and out of the garment fabric. Take the next stitch 1⁄4" (6 mm) away within the fold of the hem. Continue, keeping stitches small and 1⁄4" (6 mm) apart. The stitches will be hidden between the layers of fabric.

slant stitch: Take a tiny stitch in and out of the garment, and bring the needle through the edge of the hem. Repeat, evenly spacing and slanting the stitches. If your fabric ravels, pink the edge before hemming.

Hemming by Machine

machine blindstitch: (Refer to your owner's manual for machine settings.) Place the hem allowance facedown on the machine bed and fold back the rest of the fabric, leaving about 1⁄4" (6 mm) of the hem edge extending beyond the fold. Align the fold against the guide in the foot. Stitch along the hem, close to the fold, catching only one or two threads of the garment with each left-hand stitch. Open the fabric and press the hem flat.

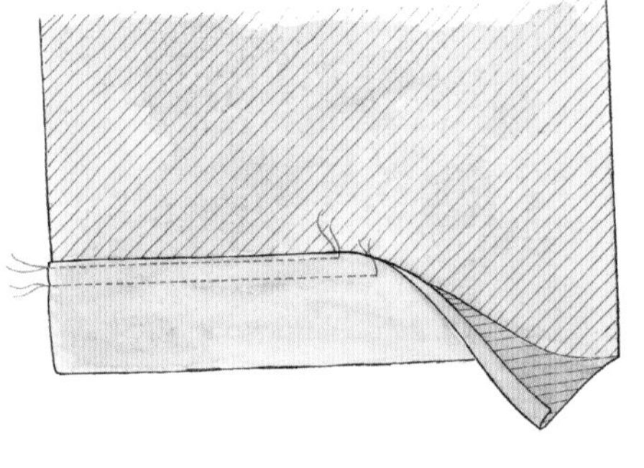

machine topstitch: Fold the hem to the desired width. Finish the edge of woven fabrics by turning under the garment edge 1⁄4" (6 mm). Press. Topstitch close to the pressed edge. You can also add a second row of stitching 1⁄4" (6 mm) away from the first.

twin needle: Hems stitched with a twin needle (see page 8) will stretch a little—so they are great for knit garments. Stitch on the right side of the fabric, catching the underside of the upper edge of the hem allowance. (You may need to buy a twin needle for your machine.)

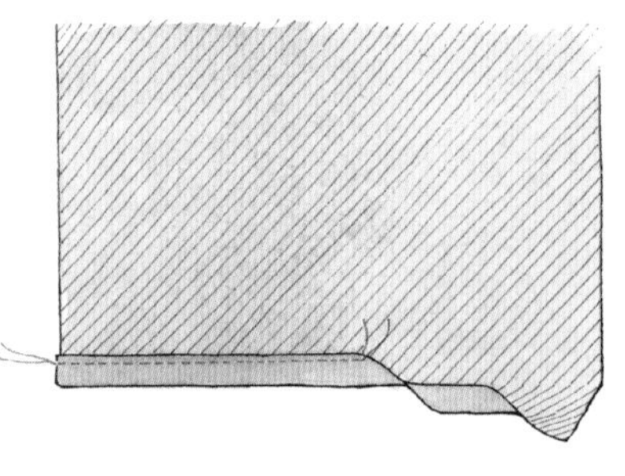

narrow hem: A narrow hem is great for sheer and silky fabrics. Trim the hem allowance to 1⁄2" (1.3 cm). Press under 1⁄4" (6 mm) and then 1⁄4" (6 mm) again. Machine-stitch close to the inner fold. This style hem is also suitable for bias-cut garments.

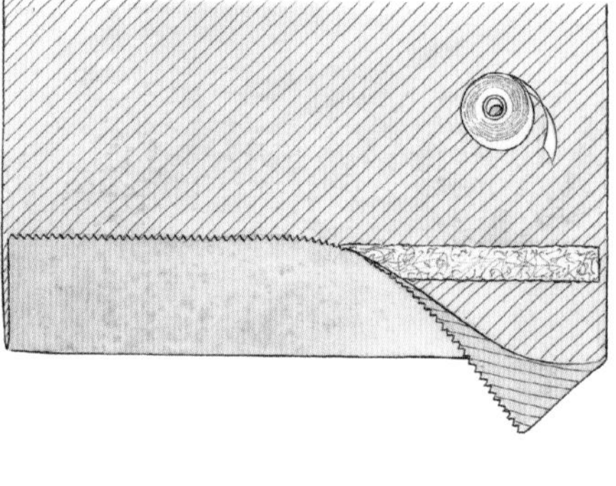

Fusing

fused hem: Hemming with fusible web is a good method for hemming lightweight woven fabrics. Test the web on scrap fabric before applying to your garment. Clean-finish the raw edge of the fabric for a neater appearance (see page 86). Insert a strip of the fusible web between the hem and the garment. Steam-press, following the manufacturer's instructions.

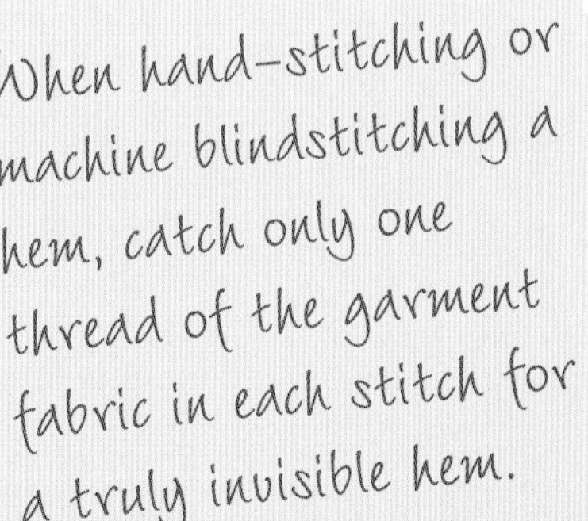

When hand-stitching or machine blindstitching a hem, catch only one thread of the garment fabric in each stitch for a truly invisible hem.

pressing pointers

- [ ] Always test the heat setting on scrap fabric first to make sure the iron is the correct temperature for your fabric.
- [ ] Press after completing each step of the construction process.
- [ ] Always use a press cloth to prevent heat shine and water spotting. A scrap of muslin makes a good press cloth.
- [ ] Seam allowances might leave an impression on the right side of delicate fabrics, so insert strips of brown paper between the seam allowances and the garment.
- [ ] Whenever possible, press on the wrong side of the fabric.
- [ ] When pressing curves, take care not to pull or stretch the fabric.
- [ ] Press seams and darts before stitching another seam across them.
- [ ] Do not press over basting threads or pins—they might leave marks in the fabric.

Careful and frequent pressing is the key to great-looking garments. Pressing is not the same process as ironing. When pressing, lift and firmly place the iron—do not glide over the fabric, as when ironing.

Pressing Straight Seams

1. Press along the stitching line to embed the stitches into the fabric.
2. Press the seam open, creasing the folds with the tip of the iron.

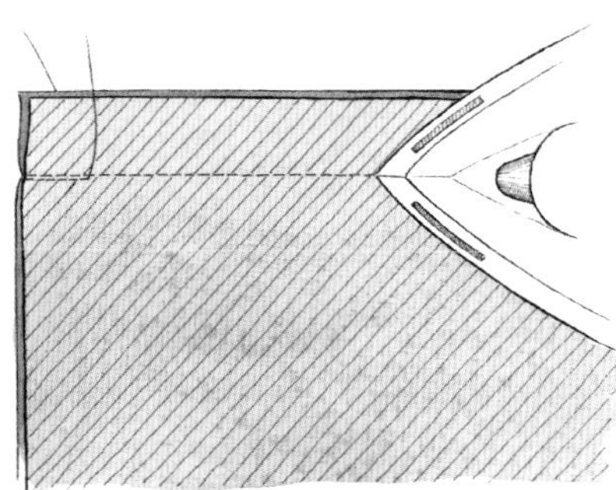

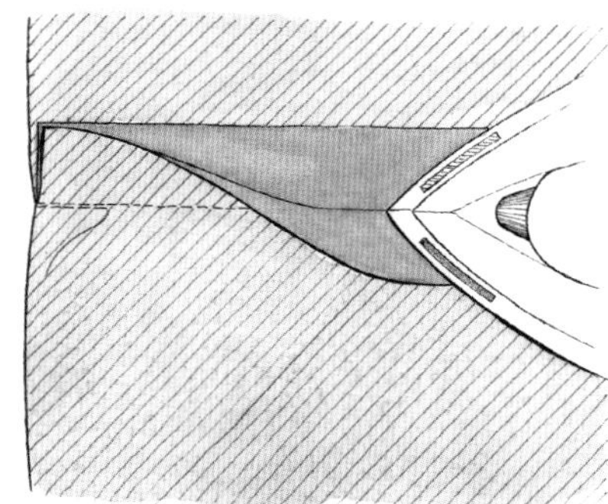

Pressing curved seams

1. Press the seam flat along the stitching line, to embed the stitches. Clip or notch the curve, as needed (see page 55).
2. Press the seam open on a tailor's ham or seam roll (see page 18), pressing with only the tip of the iron.

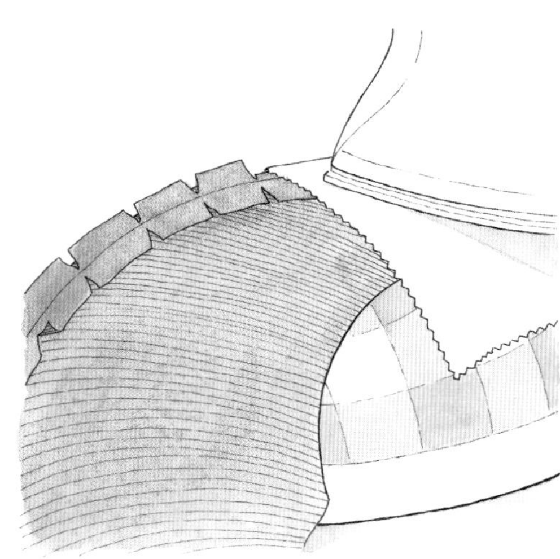

sewing stretch fabrics

The term "stretch fabrics" refers to stretch-woven fabrics, single knits, some double knits, and bias-cut fabrics (see page 101). The seams in these elastic fabrics need to stretch with the fabric, or they may pucker and stitches might break, so they need to be sewn with stitches that stretch, too. If you must sew stretch fabrics with a straight stitch, hold the fabric taut—don't pull it. Stop occasionally and, with the needle in the fabric, raise the presser foot to relax the fabric. Sew a second line of stitching 1⁄8" (3 mm) from the first.

narrow zigzag: Every machine can sew this style of stitch. Set the stitch width to a very narrow setting and the stitch length equal to the stitch width.

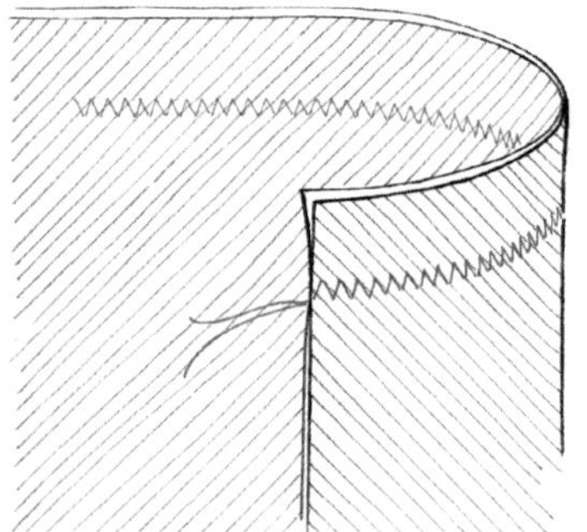

overedge stitch: This specialty stretch stitch locks over the edge of the fabric so it stitches and finishes a seam in one pass.

straight stretch stitch: This specialty stitch looks like three parallel rows of straight stitches. To create it, the machine stitches back and forth in a straight line.

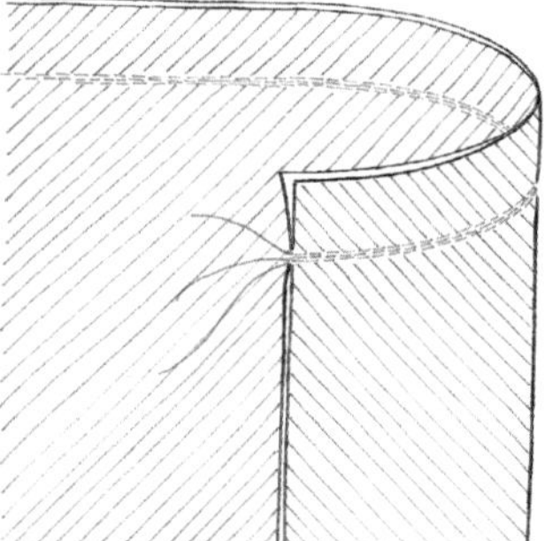

twin-needle stitch: This specialty stitch requires a twin needle. The right side of the fabric has two parallel rows of stitching. On the wrong side, the bobbin thread follows a zigzag pattern.

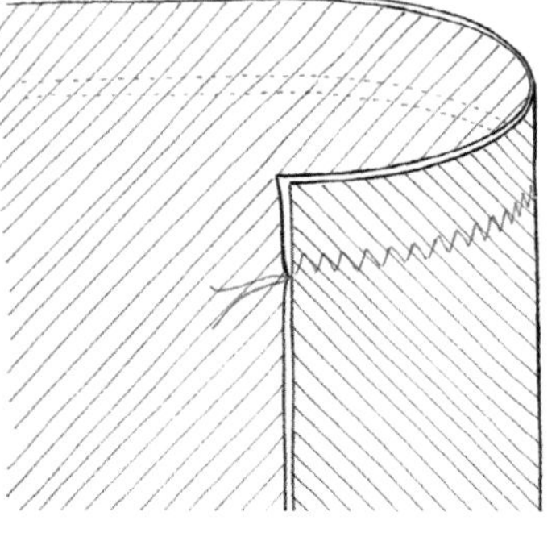

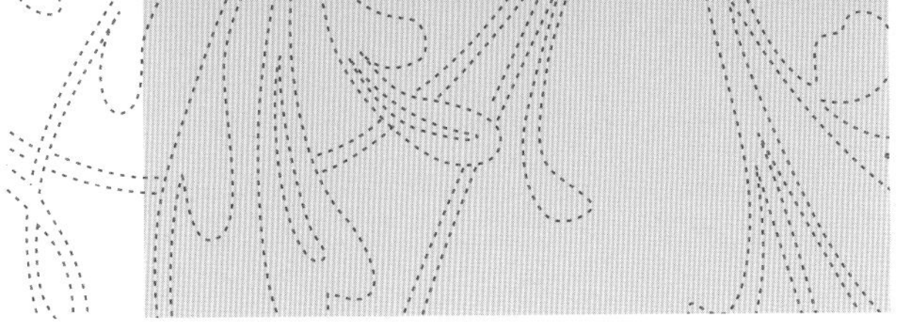

- Prewash or dry-clean the fabric, following the care instructions.
- Gently press out any creases.
- Lay out the pattern on the fabric so the most stretch wraps around the body. Follow the "with nap" layout.
- If both sides of the fabric look the same, mark one side of each cut piece as the right side with chalk or a small piece of tape.
- Stitch with a ballpoint needle, polyester thread, and a stretch stitch.
- Press carefully—don't slide the iron—to avoid stretching the fabric.
- To stabilize but not restrict the knit, apply fusible knit interfacing to collars, cuffs, pockets, plackets, and facings.

Commercial patterns that call for knit fabrics usually have a stretch gauge on the back. To test a knit, fold it crosswise and hold it up to the gauge. If it stretches to the indicated point, the fabric has enough stretch for that pattern.

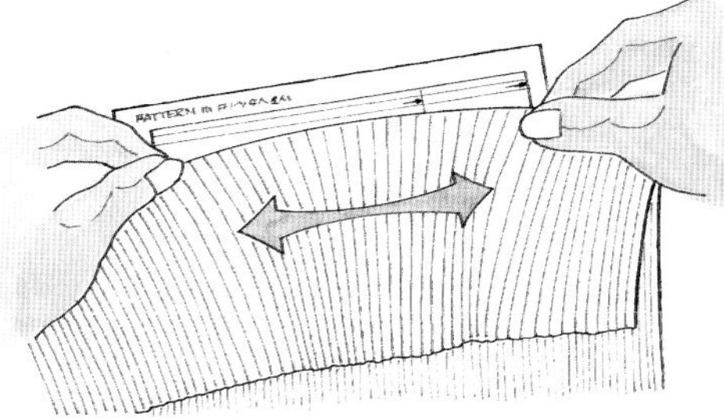

If the seam allowances tend to curl, sew a second row of stitching and trim the seam allowance close to the second row.

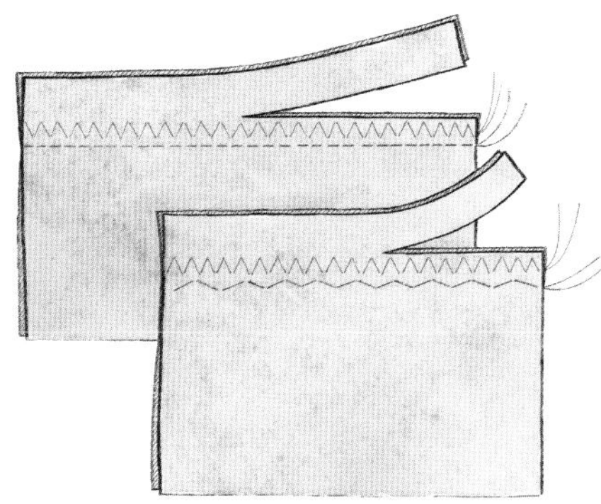

When stitching buttonholes in a stretch fabric, stitch in the direction of the least stretch. Stabilize the wrong side of the fabric first with fusible interfacing.

sewing slippery fabrics

The key to sewing slippery fabrics—silk, polyester, rayon, and acetate—is to avoid overhandling them. These delicate fabrics mar easily. Set the stitch length to between ten and fifteen stitches per inch (2.5 cm) and hold the fabric taut while stitching. You might need to loosen the thread tension and lighten the presser foot pressure slightly. Make a practice seam with a scrap piece of your fabric. Stitch with a straight-stitch presser foot or an even-feed foot (page 10) to keep the fabric from creeping.

If the fabric does creep or slip, baste the seam first by hand or use basting tape to hold the fabric in place (see page 61). Sew with plain, straight-stitch seams. If the fabric ravels, pink the seam allowances or apply liquid fray preventer to the edges. If the fabric is sheer, make French seams (page 57).

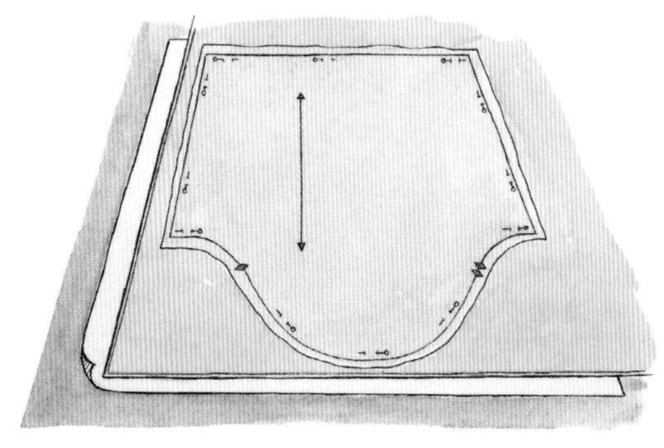

- Prewash the fabric, lining, (and interfacing, if necessary) following the fabric care instructions. Before laying out the pattern, fold the fabric right side out so the wrong sides are together.
- Follow the "with nap" layout to avoid shading variations in the finished garment.
- Use extra-fine pins or fabric weights to hold the paper pattern in place. Place pins in the seam allowances.
- If the fabric is very slippery, place tissue paper under it. Pin through the paper pattern, fabric, and tissue paper.

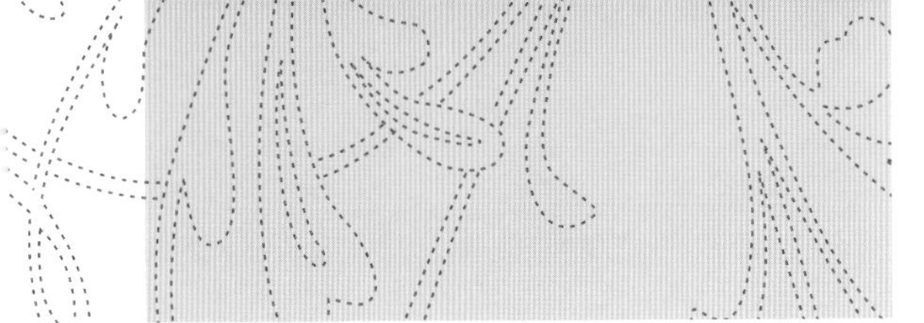

- Cut pieces with a rotary cutter to prevent the fabric from shifting.
- You can also cut with bent-handled dressmaker's shears (page 15)—one blade rests on the cutting surface. Scissors with serrated blades help grip the slippery fabric while cutting, trimming, and grading.

To find the right iron temperature for a slippery fabric, press a scrap piece of the fabric first, beginning with the iron on a low setting. Raise the temperature slowly, as needed. Use another fabric scrap for a press cloth, right side down. Don't press too hard. If the fabric is very lightweight, seam allowance edges might be visible on the right side. To avoid this, press the seams on a seam roll or slip a sheet of paper between the seam allowance and the fabric.

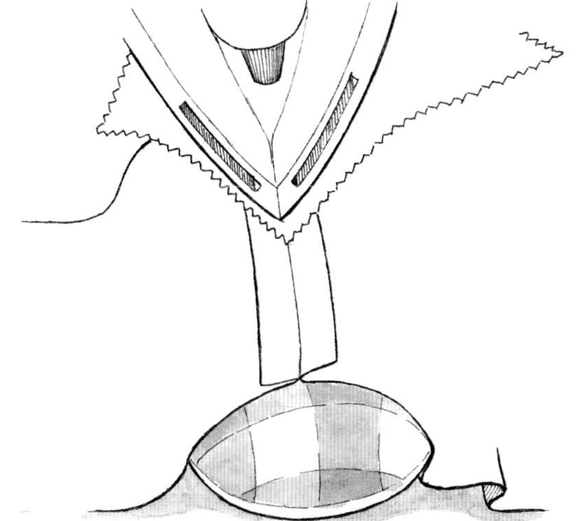

For better control when cutting slippery fabrics, cover the cutting surface with a sheet or flannel-backed vinyl tablecloth (flannel side up).

sewing sheer & lace fabrics

Sheer fabrics can be a sewing challenge. They are transparent, somewhat fragile, and have a tendency to creep. They are also beautiful and elegant, so don't let the challenges hold you back! Crisp sheers—organza, voile, organdy, and handkerchief linen—are easier to cut and sew than soft sheers and are fine for tailored items, such as shirts. Soft sheers—batiste, eyelet, chiffon, and georgette—and open weaves, such as net and lace, are better for loosely fitted garments with fewer tailored details.

Because all the seams in a sheer or lace fabric are visible from the outside, they should be narrow and neat. French seams and flat-fell seams (see pages 56 and 57) are best for these fabrics. Use short stitches (12 to 18 stitches per inch [2.5 cm]), a straight-stitch presser foot, and a straight-stitch throat plate (if you have them). Otherwise, work with a general-purpose presser foot. If the fabric still slips, try an even-feed foot (see page 10).

- Prewash the fabric, following the fabric care instructions.
- Before laying out the pattern, fold the fabric right side out, so the less slippery wrong sides are together.
- Follow the “with nap” layout if the fabric has a sheen or pattern.
- For laces and fabrics with a definite pattern, match pieces at the seams (see page 98).

- To prevent the fabric from being pulled through the throat plate at the beginning of a seam, place a small piece of stabilizer under the fabric at the beginning of the seam. Start sewing on the stabilizer and then stitch onto the fabric.
- Set the iron on a low temperature setting and increase only as needed.
- Hold both thread ends as you take the first few stitches so they don't tangle.
- Apply liquid fray preventer to the cut edges if they fray.
- Instead of backstitching, shorten the stitch at the beginning and end of the seam or knot the threads.
- To prevent puckers, place tear-away stabilizer or tissue paper under the fabric and stitch through all layers. Remove the paper carefully so you don't distort the stitches.

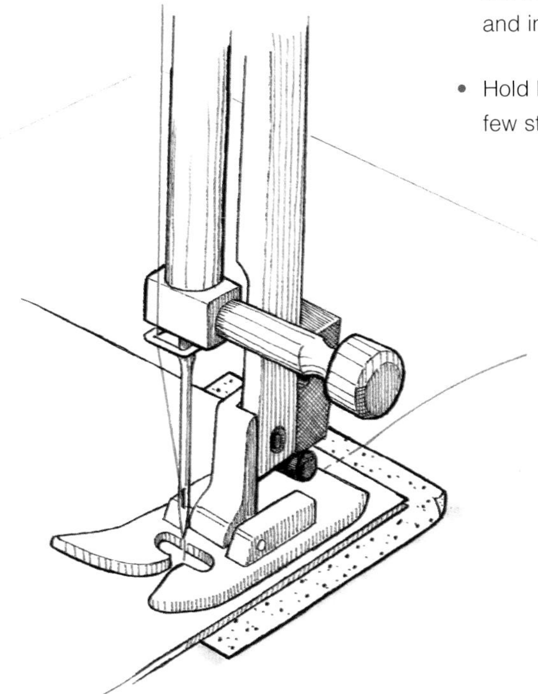

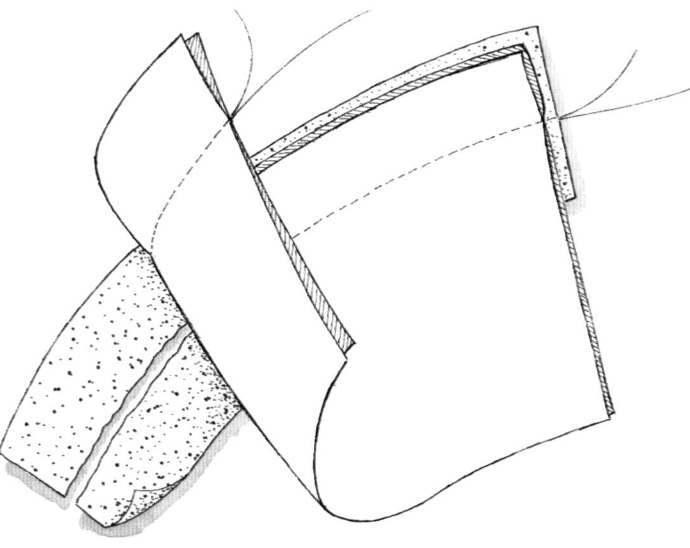

sewing napped fabrics

Nap refers to the raised fibers on the surface of a fabric. These fibers naturally run one direction or the other. On pile fabrics, such as corduroy or velvet, you can feel the nap. Fleece, faux fur, suede, leather, brushed cotton, some knits, terry, and velveteen are all napped fabrics.

Rub your hand along the surface of the fabric. If the fabric feels rough, the nap is running in the opposite direction—you are rubbing "against" the nap. If the fabric feels smooth, you are rubbing "with" the nap. In this direction, the fabric surface is also lighter and shinier.

- It is sometimes easier to cut napped (especially pile) fabric in a single layer, as you would for striped fabrics (see page 99). Make sure to flip the pattern pieces when you lay out the second set, so that you have both right and left sides.

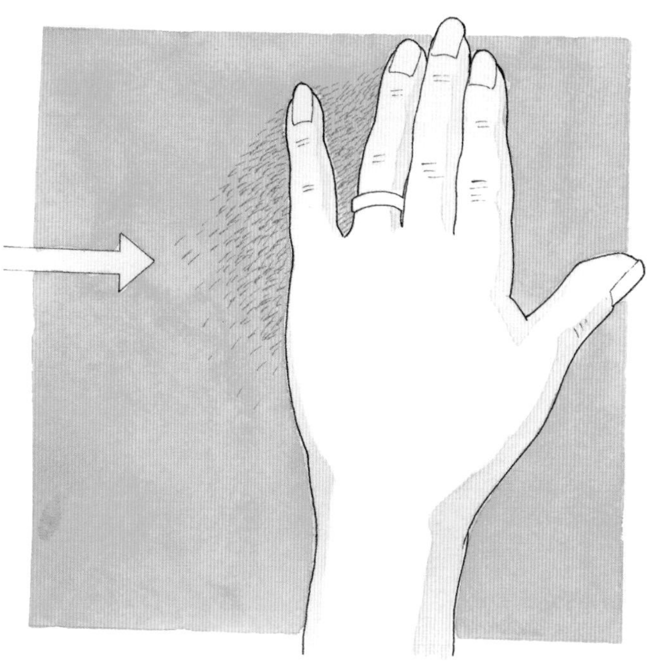

- Stitch with a standard, straight seam. For heavier fabrics, use longer stitches—about 5 to 8 stitches per inch (2.5 cm).
- Hold the fabric taut when stitching, and whenever possible, stitch in the same direction as the nap.
- For fabrics that ravel, overedge-stitch or pink the edges (pages 58 and 59).
- Avoid seam finishes that add bulk.
- To press, place the fabric facedown on a needleboard, terry towel, or a piece of the same fabric, so you don't crush the pile.

It is important to cut all the pattern pieces in the same direction, or "with the nap." Deciding which direction to place the pattern pieces is a matter of personal taste. Either way is fine as long as you are consistent.

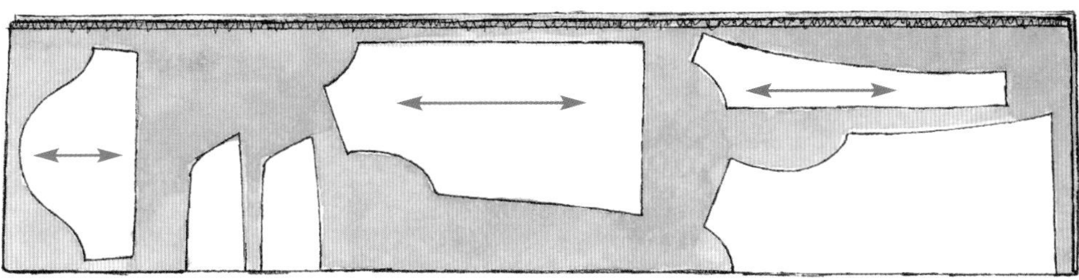

To reduce bulk on heavy pile fabrics, such as faux fur, trim away the extra fibers from the seam allowances.

sewing striped, plaid & print fabrics

Plaids, stripes, and prints are strong visual patterns, so it is important to match them at prominent seams. If you are careful laying and cutting out the pattern, the seams will be almost invisible. You need to buy extra fabric, 1/4 to 1/2 yard (0.25 to 0.5 m), depending on the size of the pattern repeat (the distance from one bar of the plaid or stripe to the next identical bar or from one large motif to another). The larger the repeat, the more extra fabric you need.

Small-scale and overall prints do not require pattern matching, so they are easier to lay out and cut. Lay out fabrics with a border print (a prominent design along the selvage) so the pattern falls at a center front opening or runs along the garment hem. Choose simple style garments and avoid any pattern that says it is not suitable for plaids or stripes.

To keep seams from shifting while sewing . . .

- pin frequently
- hand-baste or use basting tape
- use a walking foot

Laying Out Pattern Pieces

Open the fabric in a single layer, right side up. Trace pattern pieces that need both a right and a left side. If a piece is to be cut on the fold, abut the right and left pieces together, as shown in the drawing below, at left.

Center the front and back pattern pieces on a prominent color bar or motif. Carefully align the side seam notches. Match the pattern pieces at stitching lines, not cutting lines.

Center the sleeve on the same prominent color bar or motif as the front and back. Align the front armhole notches of the sleeve and the garment front.

Position smaller pieces, such as yokes, plackets, or patch pockets, on the true bias (45 degrees to the grain) or position them so the plaid, stripe, or print motifs will match the larger garment pieces.

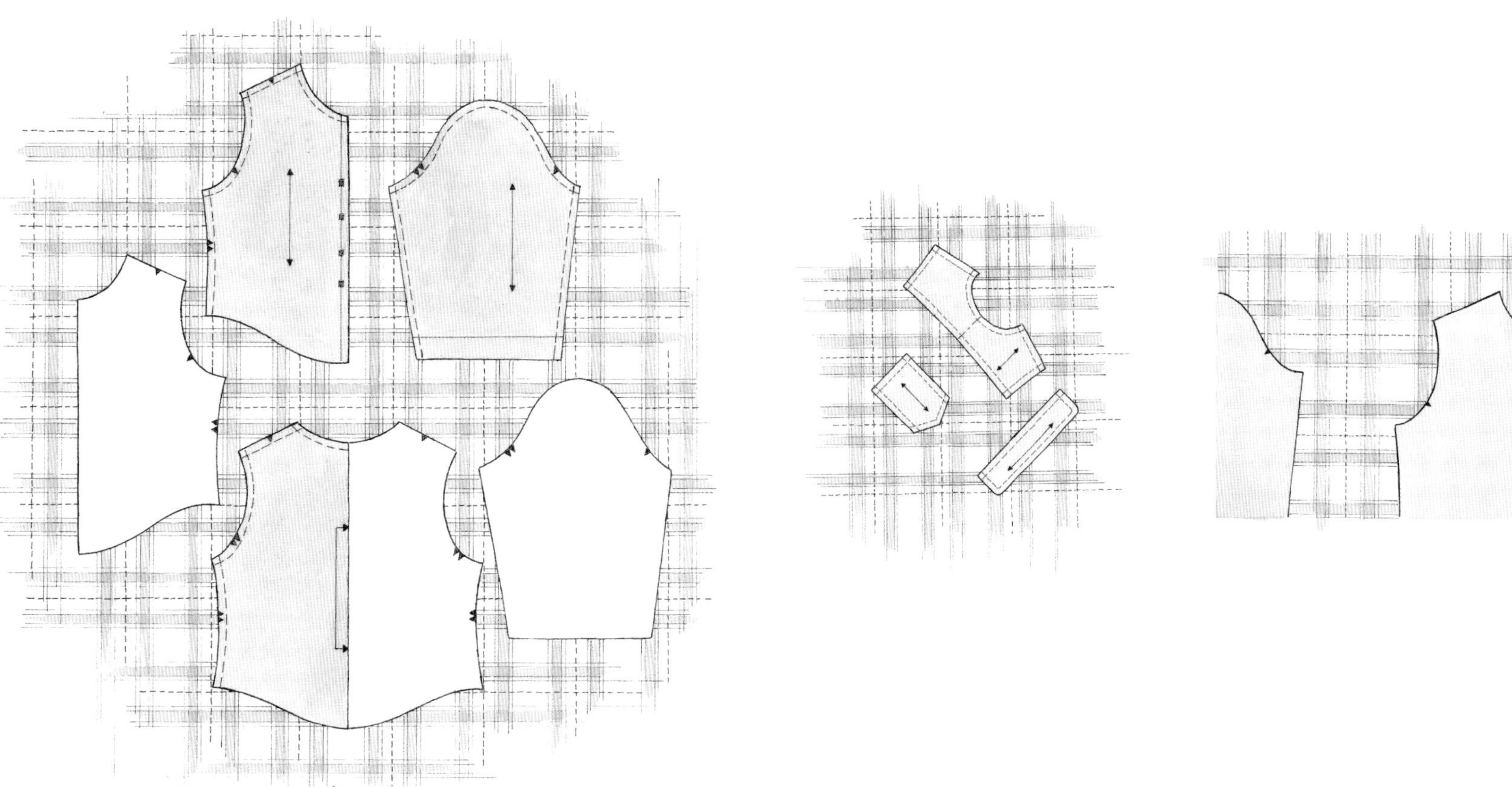

woven fabrics

Most fabrics are woven. There are several weave patterns, created by the interlacing of lengthwise (warp) and crosswise (weft) yarns. If the yarn strands are dyed before weaving, the fabric has consistent color on both sides. If not, the fabric is printed to create a patterned right side and a mottled or solid-color wrong side.

plain weave: Plain-weave fabrics are flat, smooth, and easy to sew. They wrinkle but do not ravel excessively. They don't drape well and are difficult to ease. Muslin, taffeta, percale, and wool challis are plain-weave fabrics.

rib weave: Rib weave is a variation of plain weave, with one yarn thicker than the other. The fabric tends to slip during stitching and is weaker than plain weave. Rib-weave fabrics, which include poplin, faille, and ottoman, may require a "with nap" layout.

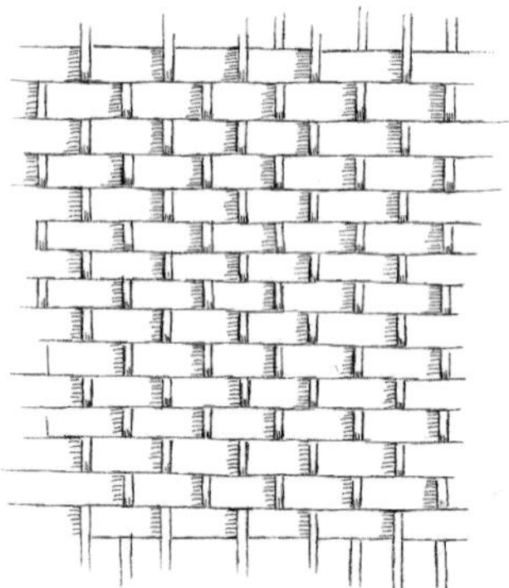

satin weave: Satin-weave fabrics have a characteristic surface sheen because the warp yarns float over several weft yarns. The fabrics have a lustrous surface, snag easily, and are marred by pins and needles. They ravel excessively and slip during stitching. Antique satin, charmeuse, crepe-back satin, and sateen are all satin-weave fabrics.

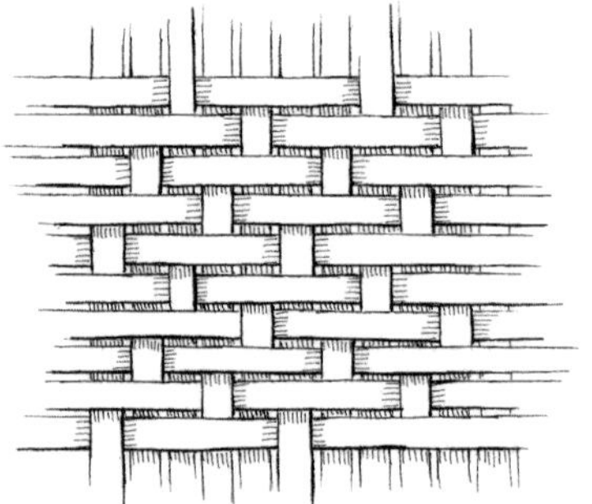

twill weave: Twill-weave fabrics appear to have diagonal lines on the surface. These sometimes-bulky fabrics are strong, durable, heavy, and wrinkle resistant. They tend to fray, abrade at edges, and may require a "with nap" layout. Denim, serge, ticking, and gabardine have a twill-weave structure.

knit fabrics

Knit fabrics are formed by a series of interlocking loops. Although they may differ in their weight, texture, and fiber content, all knits are stretchy, comfortable, wrinkle resistant, and easy to sew. Most should be sewn with stitches that stretch with the fabric (see page 90). Cut edges don't ravel, so seam allowances usually don't need to be finished. Some knits may shrink, depending on their fiber content. Some might require a "with nap" layout.

single knits: Single knits are made with a single set of needles so there are knit stitches on front, purl stitches on back. These fabrics are stretchy and best suited for close-fitting garments with few construction details. Crosswise-cut edges can run, and lengthwise-cut edges can curl.

double knits: Double-knit fabrics are made with two sets of needles, so the fabric has the same knit structure and appearance on both sides. Double knits are stable, with very little stretch, so they hold their shape well.

stable knits: Stable knit fabrics have limited stretch or none at all. They are generally not suitable for "knits only" patterns. Garments made with stable knits don't need stretch seams. The fabric won't curl at the edges or ravel.

moderate and two-way: Moderate-stretch knits stretch lengthwise but not crosswise. Two-way stretch knits stretch both lengthwise and crosswise, which makes them suitable for active sportswear. Garments made with moderate-stretch or two-way-stretch knit fabric need to have stretch seams (see page 90).

Knit Characteristics

- [ ] elastic
- [ ] comfortable fit
- [ ] wrinkle resistant
- [ ] easy to sew

cotton

Most cotton fabrics are easy to sew—great for beginners and expert sewers, too. Cotton is the most popular fiber in the world. It comes from the seedpod of the cotton plant. The fiber can be knit or woven and is manufactured in many different weights and weaves.

Characteristics	Care Requirements	Types of Cotton Fabric
• very absorbent • comfortable to wear year-round • easy to launder, but soils easily • dyes well, retains color • strong, durable • very flammable • resists abrasion, pilling, and damage from moths • wrinkles easily • tendency to shrink • exposure to sunlight weakens fibers	• Cotton can be laundered at high water temperature with soap and water. • Fibers tend to pick up dirt, so should be washed frequently. • Cotton shrinks more in hot water than cold, so unless garment is very soiled, wash in cold water. • Loose weaves shrink more than tight weaves, so should be dry-cleaned.	• **batiste:** soft and lightweight; suitable for lingerie, blouses, baby dresses • **broadcloth:** light to medium weight; suitable for sportswear, shirts, pajamas • **corduroy:** pile fabric, very durable; suitable for pants, casual sportswear • **denim:** strong, durable fabric; suitable for jeans and work pants • **flannel:** very soft with slight nap on one or both sides • **lace:** textured fabric with open pattern • **muslin:** inexpensive fabric; often used for crafts and sample garments • **sateen:** shiny and lustrous; often used for formalwear

linen

Linen fibers are obtained from the stem of the flax plant. The fabric is luxurious, but expensive to produce, and wrinkles easily. It is also two times as strong as 100 percent cotton and five times as strong as 100 percent wool! Traditionally a warm-weather fabric, linen is ideal for summer dresses, shirts, and slacks.

Characteristics	Care Requirements	Types of Linen Fabric
• absorbent and cool in warm weather • natural luster • quick-drying • retains shape well • sheds surface dirt, stain resistant • yellows with age • wrinkles easily • frays easily • shrinks • poor elasticity • develops shine if pressed without a press cloth	• Dry-clean linen garments because they wrinkle and lose their trademark crispness in the wash. • If you intend to wash the finished item, preshrink it in the washing machine before cutting. • If you intend to dry-clean, steam-press the fabric before cutting. • Machine-wash in gentle cycle and cool water and dry on a regular heat setting. • Remove from dryer while still damp and immediately press on the wrong side, or with a press cloth, at a high temperature.	• **damask:** reversible with elaborate designs woven into the cloth • **handkerchief linen:** very lightweight; ideal for lingerie, baby clothes, dresses, and blouses • **lawn:** very fine, lightweight, and closely woven; suitable for fine lingerie, dresses, and collars • **linen:** any weight of strong, lustrous, and absorbent fabric made from the flax plant

silk

Silk is sometimes called the queen of fibers. It has a soft hand (tactile quality), beautiful drape, and unique luster. Silkworms produce silk as they spin their cocoons, and the fiber is cultivated mostly in Asia and China. It takes about 600 silkworm cocoons to make enough fabric for a shirt.

Silk fibers are knitted and woven into lightweight fabrics, such as crepe de chine, suitable for eveningwear, and crisp fabrics suitable for tailored jackets. Light, slippery silks benefit from special sewing techniques (see page 92).

Characteristics	Care Requirements	Types of Silk Fabric
• natural luster • absorbent and cool in warm weather • insulating in cold weather • strong and long lasting • resilient, doesn't wrinkle easily • resists shrinking and stretching • dyes well; some bold colors fade or lose dye when washed • may stain with perspiration and water • expensive • difficult to care for • sometimes requires special sewing techniques	• Dry-clean silk garments with loose weaves, bold colors, heavy weight, and a lot of tailoring or construction details. • Hand-wash small, lightweight garments in warm water with mild detergent. Roll the garment in a towel to remove excess water and lay out on a second towel to dry. • Iron the garment on the wrong side while it's still damp, using a press cloth. • To test washability, prewash a small scrap. After it dries, check to make sure the color, texture, and luster didn't change. • Never spot-clean silk; water may leave a permanent mark.	• **charmeuse:** soft with lustrous face and dull back; drapes well • **chiffon:** lightweight and transparent; suitable for eveningwear • **crepe de chine:** light to medium weight; suitable for dresses, blouses, lingerie, and eveningwear • **doupioni:** uneven surface with yarn slubs, ravels easily; suitable for suits and dresses • **peau de soie:** dull surface, satin weave; suitable for bridal gowns and eveningwear • **shantung:** dull or lustrous finish with irregular yarns and surface slubs; suitable for suits, dresses, slacks, and blouses • **taffeta:** smooth and crisp, with characteristic rustle as it moves; suitable for dresses and eveningwear

wool

Wool comes from the fleece of sheep and lambs. More specialized fabrics come from angora, cashmere goat, camel, alpaca, llama, and vicuña. Wool has a medium luster and is manufactured in all weights, for all types of garments. It is easy to sew and care for.

There are two basic types of wool fibers. Woolens are soft with a fuzzy texture. The more expensive, lightweight worsteds are smooth, strong, and lustrous and they wear and press well.

Characteristics	Care Requirements	Types of Wool Fabric
• long lasting • easy-care finishes • absorbent • stain and moisture repellent • resilient (stretches up to 35 percent when dry and 50 percent when wet) • comfortable in all kinds of weather • shrinks and felts when washed • susceptible to insect damage • coarse fibers may irritate skin • expensive • wrinkle resistant • develops shine if pressed without a press cloth	• Dry-clean. Wool does not need to be laundered as frequently as other fabrics. • Brush and hang wool garments immediately after wearing. • Sponge the garment periodically to remove surface dirt. • Treat stains immediately with a mild solution of soap and water. • Launder washable wools (check the end of the bolt) in cool water with mild detergent and lay flat to dry to retain shape. • Press with a press cloth to avoid shine.	• **blanket cloth:** heavily napped for warmth; suitable for coats, jackets, and bathrobes • **bouclé:** loops or curls on the surface; suitable for dresses and suits • **challis:** great drapability, gathers well, often printed; suitable for dresses, skirts, and scarves • **crepe:** dull, crinkled surface in variety of weights; suitable for dresses, skirts, and slacks • **flannel:** lightly napped surface; great for slacks, jackets, and suits • **gabardine:** firm, twill-weave, worsted wool; durable; suitable for slacks, suits, dresses, and jackets • **serge:** worsted wool; suitable for tailored suits and trousers • **tweed:** rough with slubs and nubs on the surface; yarn-dyed tweed has flecked appearance; suitable for jackets, slacks, and skirts • **wool jersey:** comfortable, lightweight knit fabric that drapes well; suitable for sportswear and dresses

rayon, acetate & triacetate

Rayon, acetate, and triacetate are made from plant cellulose (cotton waste, wood pulp) that is pushed through spinnerettes (metal plates with tiny holes). Variations in the process produce three distinct fiber types. The fabrics resemble cotton, linen, wool, and silk. Sewing ease depends on the weave and surface of the actual fabric.

Rayon Characteristics	Acetate Characteristics	Triacetate Characteristics	Care Requirements	Types of Fabrics
• drapes beautifully • absorbent and cool • soft, comfortable to wear • easy to dye • blends well with other fibers • loses strength when wet • ravels easily • shrinks, poor shape retention • poor resiliency, wrinkles easily • fades from exposure to light	• high luster • drapes well • resists mildew and mold • poor resiliency, wrinkles easily • subject to abrasion • sensitive to high heat, melts	• drapes well • high luster • poor durability and elasticity • wrinkle resistant • can be permanently heat-set, good pleat and crease retention • often blended with cotton and rayon	• Dry-clean rayon and acetate or hand-wash with mild detergent and water. Remove excess water by rolling the garment in a towel and then dry on a plastic hanger. Press on the wrong side with press cloth while the fabric is damp. • Hand-wash or machine-wash triacetate and air- or machine-dry.	• **challis (rayon):** soft, firm fabric, often printed with small, overall design; suitable for dresses, skirts, and scarves • **faille (acetate):** flat rib surface; dressy fabric for dresses, jackets, and coats • **satin (rayon or acetate):** firmly woven with smooth surface; suitable for eveningwear and bridal gowns • **taffeta (rayon or acetate):** smooth and crisp, rustles as it moves; suitable for eveningwear • **velour (triacetate):** thick, short pile; suitable for robes and active sportswear

synthetic fibers

This group of fibers includes acrylic, nylon, polyester, and spandex. They are completely synthetic and are made from combined molecules of carbon, hydrogen, nitrogen, and oxygen. Because of modern production methods and special finishes, all of these fibers compete well—and are often blended—with natural fibers.

Microfibers, are finer versions of the man-made fibers, most often polyester. They can be one hundred times finer than human hair and one-half the diameter of fine silk fibers. They produce very soft, luxurious fabrics with easy-care properties.

Acrylic Types and Characteristics	Nylon Types and Characteristics	Polyester Types and Characteristics	Spandex Types and Characteristics	Care Requirements
(fake fur, fleece, knits, pile fabrics, some sheers) • soft, warm, and lightweight • developed as a substitute for wool • wrinkle resistant • nonabsorbent, but quick drying • moth, mold, and mildew resistant • prone to pilling • shrinks • can be heat-set into permanent pleats and creases	*(plisse, sheers, velvet, microfiber)* • very strong, resistant to wear and tear • elastic • water repellent • colorfast, easy to dye • tends to cause skipped stitches and puckered seams • pills and frays easily • can be damaged by hot iron • wrinkle resistant	*(almost any fabric type, either 100 percent polyester or blended with other fibers)* • crisp, resilient, and wrinkle resistant • good elasticity, good shape retention • easy to launder by machine, wash and wear • moth, mold, and mildew resistant • tends to cause skipped stitches and puckered seams • dulls needles and scissors • damaged by high heat • poor absorbency • pills and attracts lint • accepts dye well, colorfast • blends well with natural fibers	*(blended with other fibers to add elasticity)* • extremely elastic, stretches more than 500 percent without breaking • adds stretch to other fibers • improves fit, comfort, and shape retention in foundation garments and exercise clothing • tends to cause skipped stitches and puckered seams • easily damaged by high heat • requires special sewing techniques	• Synthetic fabrics can be machine-washed and machine-dried at low temperature. • These fabrics have a fairly low melting point, so press carefully. • Launder blended fabrics according to the care requirements of each of the fiber types. (For instance, a silk and polyester blend might need to be hand-washed to avoid water-staining the silk fibers.)

index

index

index

index